CLASSIC CHINESE

CLASSIC CHINESE

OVER 140 AUTHENTIC RECIPES SHOWN IN 250 EVOCATIVE PHOTOGRAPHS

DANNY CHAN

southwater

This edition is published by Southwater,
an imprint of Anness Publishing Ltd,
Blaby Road, Wigston, Leicestershire
LE18 4SE; info@anness.com

www.southwaterbooks.com;
www.annesspublishing.com

If you like the images in this book and would
like to investigate using them for publishing,
promotions or advertising, please visit our
website www.practicalpictures.com
for more information.

A CIP catalogue record for this book is
available from the British Library.

Publisher: Joanna Lorenz
Editor: Daniel Hurst
Designer: Ian Sandom
Jacket Designer: Sarah Rock
Indexer: Ann Barrett
Production Controller: Mai-Ling Collyer

PUBLISHER'S NOTE
Although the advice and information in this
book are believed to be accurate and true at
the time of going to press, neither the authors
nor the publisher can accept any legal
responsibility or liability for any errors or
omissions that may have been made nor for
any inaccuracies nor for any loss, harm or
injury that comes about from following
instructions or advice in this book.

NOTES
Bracketed terms are intended for
American readers.
For all recipes, quantities are given in
both metric and imperial measures and,
where appropriate, in standard cups and
spoons. Follow one set of measures, but
not a mixture, because they are not
interchangeable.
Standard spoon and cup measures are
level. 1 tsp = 5ml, 1 tbsp = 15ml, 1 cup
= 250ml/8fl oz.
Australian standard tablespoons are
20ml. Australian readers should use
3 tsp in place of 1 tbsp for measuring
small quantities.
American pints are 16fl oz/2 cups.
American readers should use 20fl oz/
2.5 cups in place of 1 pint when
measuring liquids.
Electric oven temperatures in this book
are for conventional ovens. When using
a fan oven, the temperature will
probably need to be reduced by about
10–20°C/20–40°F. Since ovens vary, you
should check with your manufacturer's
instruction book for guidance.
The nutritional analysis given for each
recipe is calculated per portion (i.e.
serving or item), unless otherwise stated.
If the recipe gives a range, such as
Serves 4–6, then the nutritional analysis
will be for the smaller portion size, i.e.
6 servings. The analysis does not include
optional ingredients, such as salt added
to taste.
Medium (US large) eggs are used unless
otherwise stated.
Front cover shows Stir-fried Squid with
Ginger – for recipe, see page 106.

Contents

Introduction

Chinese restaurants offering vast ranges of delicious, aromatic dishes are popular the world over, however, authentic Chinese food can be simple and very rewarding to make at home. This book is a celebration of the food and cooking of China, and offers an ideal gateway into this unique cuisine.

If you've ever been impressed by the range of dishes on offer at a Chinese restaurant, you'll be overwhelmed by what this book has to offer – over 150 delicious recipes for every occasion, from simple snacks to stylish desserts. Many of the dishes will be familiar, including classics like Crispy Wonton Soup, Steamed Pork Buns, Crispy Salt

BELOW: *Chinese cooking puts an emphasis on fresh and aromatic ingredients prepared simply.*

and Pepper Squid, Peking Duck with Mandarin Pancakes, and Sweet and Sour Pork. Others are less well known, but the superb colour photographs of the finished dishes will tempt you try such specialities as Chinese Fish Ball Soup, Radish Cake, Steamed Fish with Five Willow Sauce, and Pancakes with Red Bean Paste.

China is a vast country with several distinctly different cuisines. From the south comes Cantonese cooking, characterized by subtle yet

sophisticated sauces and restrained use of spices. Sweet and sour dishes come from this region, and snack foods, including dim sum pastries and dumplings, are a speciality. You can create your own feast of dim sum with a number of dishes from the Appetizers & Dim Sum chapter of this book, including tantalizing treats such as Chive Dumplings, Crab Tofu Parcels, Minced Pork and Taro Puffs, and Chilli and Pak Choi Omelette Parcels.

ABOVE: *Snacks and dim sum, like this Yam Cake, can be combined to create a delicious feast of texture and flavour.*

ABOVE: *Some Chinese dishes, including Peking Duck with Mandarin Pancakes, have become family favourites the world over.*

ABOVE: *Some authentic dishes, such as these Toffee Apples, challenge the western view of typical Chinese cuisine.*

In the east, dishes tend to be sweeter. This applies to meat and poultry as well as the grain-based foods for which the area is well known. By contrast, Sichuan cooking is hot and spicy. Liberal use of chillies, Sichuan peppercorns, garlic and onions make for dishes like Sichuan Chicken with Kung Po Sauce, which pack a pleasurable punch. Striking contrasts in flavours are also a feature and can be experienced in Hot and Sour Soup and Duck and Preserved Lime Soup. In the north, where winters are hard and cold, ribsticking stews are favoured, as are dishes like Mongolian Firepot and Chinese Braised Pork Belly with Asian Greens.

The biggest challenge could be in choosing just what to make first. It might be Egg Knot Soup, delicate and pretty, or a nourishing bowl of Beef Noodle Soup. Perhaps you are craving a light snack, like Spiced Noodle Pancakes or Pork and Peanut Wontons with Plum Sauce. Vegetarians are well catered for, with such delights as Marinated Tofu and Broccoli with Crispy Fried Shallots, Chinese Steamed Winter Melon with Barley and Sesame-tossed Asparagus with Bean Thread Noodles providing a welcome change from more prosaic choices. If fish or shellfish is what is fancied, try Lobster Noodles, Braised Grouper in Black Bean Sauce or Mackerel with Shiitake Mushrooms and Black Beans.

In all its many guises, Chinese food has become immensely popular throughout the world, with the result that once-scarce ingredients are now commonplace. Fresh root ginger is to be found in every supermarket and even lemon grass and galangal are widely available. You can now also obtain fresh shiitake, oyster and enoki mushrooms. Sauces are a staple of Chinese cooking, and it is not difficult to find several kinds of soy sauce, as well as black and yellow bean sauces, oyster, mushroom, hoisin and plum sauces. Noodles and spring roll wrappers are also on sale everywhere, so finding what you need to make the dishes in this collection should never prove a problem. All of these ingredients are explored in a dedicated section at the close of this book, which will equip you with all the knowledge you need to embark on creating delicious and authentic Chinese meals.

Soups & broths

Ranging from simple, aromatic broths through to substantial dishes that make delicious meals in their own right, this chapter presents a range of tempting soups for any occasion. The recipes include tasty traditional classics such as Crispy Wonton Soup and Hot and Sour Soup, as well as exotic and unusual offerings such as Duck and Preserved Lime Soup.

Egg flower soup

This simple, healthy soup is flavoured with fresh root ginger and Chinese five-spice powder. It is quick and delicious and can be made at the last minute.

SERVES 4

1.2 litres/2 pints/5 cups fresh chicken or
   vegetable stock
10ml/2 tsp peeled, grated fresh
   root ginger
10ml/2 tsp light soy sauce
5ml/1 tsp sesame oil
5ml/1 tsp five-spice powder
15–30ml/1–2 tbsp cornflour (cornstarch)
2 eggs
salt and ground black pepper
1 spring onion (scallion), very finely
   sliced diagonally, and 15ml/1 tbsp
   roughly chopped coriander (cilantro)
   or flat leaf parsley, to garnish

1 Put the chicken or vegetable stock into a large pan with the ginger, soy sauce, oil and five-spice powder. Bring to the boil and allow to simmer gently for about 10 minutes.

2 Blend the cornflour in a measuring jug (cup) with 60–75ml/4–5 tbsp water and stir into the stock. Cook, stirring constantly, until slightly thickened. Season with salt and pepper.

3 In a jug (pitcher), beat the eggs together with 30ml/2 tbsp cold water until the mixture becomes frothy.

4 Bring the soup back just to the boil and drizzle in the egg mixture, stirring vigorously with chopsticks. Choose a jug with a fine spout to form a very thin drizzle. Serve at once, sprinkled with the sliced spring onions and chopped coriander or parsley.

Nutritional information per portion: Energy 58kcal/244kJ; Protein 3.3g; Carbohydrate 3.8g, of which sugars 0.3g; Fat 3.6g, of which saturates 0.9g; Cholesterol 95mg; Calcium 16mg; Fibre 0g; Sodium 304mg.

Rice congee

This Chinese dish has spread throughout South-east Asia and is loved for its simplicity. It is teamed with strongly flavoured accompaniments to provide contrasting tastes and textures.

SERVES 2

900ml/1¹/₂ pints/3³/₄ cups
   vegetable stock
200g/7oz cooked rice
15ml/1 tbsp fish sauce,
   or mushroom ketchup
2 heads pickled garlic, finely chopped
1 celery stick, finely diced
ground black pepper

TO GARNISH

4 garlic cloves
4 small red shallots
30ml/2 tbsp groundnut (peanut) oil

1 To make the garnishes, thinly slice the garlic cloves and the shallots. Heat the groundnut oil in a wok and cook the garlic and shallots over a low heat until brown. Drain on kitchen paper and reserve for the soup.

2 Pour the vegetable stock into a wok or large pan. Bring to the boil and add the rice.

3 Stir in the Thai fish sauce or mushroom ketchup and pickled garlic and simmer for 10 minutes to let the flavours develop, then stir in the finely diced celery.

4 Serve the rice congee in individual warmed bowls. Sprinkle over the prepared garlic and shallots and season each bowl with plenty of ground pepper.

Nutritional information per portion: Energy 509kcal/2126kJ; Protein 27.3g; Carbohydrate 37.2g, of which sugars 0.8g; Fat 29g, of which saturates 6.3g; Cholesterol 74mg; Calcium 39mg; Fibre 1.8g; Sodium 86mg.

Cellophane noodle soup

Exotic dried lily flowers are popular in China. These edible flowers are also known as 'tiger lily buds' or 'golden needles', and are used in a variety of soups and other dishes.

SERVES 4

4 large dried shiitake mushrooms
15g/1/2oz dried lily buds
1/2 cucumber, coarsely chopped
2 garlic cloves, halved
90g/31/2oz white cabbage, chopped
1.2 litres/2 pints/5 cups boiling water
115g/4oz cellophane noodles
30ml/2 tbsp soy sauce
15ml/1 tbsp palm sugar (jaggery)
    or light muscovado (brown) sugar
90g/31/2oz block silken tofu, diced
fresh coriander (cilantro) leaves,
    to garnish

1 In separate bowls, soak the dried lily buds and mushrooms in warm water for 30 minutes.

2 Put the cucumber, garlic and cabbage in a food processor and process to a paste. Scrape into a large pan and add the boiling water.

3 Bring to the boil, then reduce the heat and cook for 2 minutes. Strain the stock into another pan, return to a low heat and bring to a simmer.

4 Drain the lily buds, rinse under cold running water, then drain again. Cut off any hard ends. Add to the stock with the noodles, soy sauce and sugar and cook for 5 minutes more.

5 Strain the mushroom soaking liquid into the soup. Discard the mushroom stems, then slice the caps. Divide them and the tofu among four bowls. Pour the soup over, garnish and serve.

Nutritional information per portion: Energy 148kcal/618kJ; Protein 4.1g; Carbohydrate 29.7g, of which sugars 5.7g; Fat 1.1g, of which saturates 0.1g; Cholesterol 0mg; Calcium 139mg; Fibre 0.7g; Sodium 546mg.

Egg drop and ginger soup

This soup is very easy to make, nutritious and beautifully light; the sort of thing that would be served at home to refresh the palate between more elaborate dishes.

SERVES 4

750ml/1¼ pints/3 cups fresh
    vegetable stock
30ml/2 tbsp fresh root ginger,
    finely shredded
2 eggs
30ml/2 tbsp rice wine
chopped spring onions (scallions)
    or fresh coriander (cilantro),
    to garnish

1 Bring the stock to the boil in a medium pan. Add the finely shredded ginger and cook for 3 minutes.

2 Beat the eggs and pour them into the soup in a steady stream, using a fork to stir the surface. As it cooks, the egg will set, forming long strands.

3 Stir in the rice wine. Ladle into bowls, garnish with the spring onions or coriander, and serve hot.

VARIATION
For more substance, add cellophane noodles to the soup just before the egg.

Nutritional information per portion: Energy 44kcal/184kJ; Protein 3.3g; Carbohydrate 0.2g, of which sugars 0.1g; Fat 2.9g, of which saturates 0.8g; Cholesterol 95mg; Calcium 18mg; Fibre 0.1g; Sodium 166mg.

Omelette soup

A very satisfying soup that is quick and easy to prepare. It is versatile, too, in that you can vary the vegetables according to what is available in the season.

SERVES 4

1 egg
15ml/1 tbsp groundnut
    (peanut) oil
900ml/1½ pints/3¾ cups
    well-flavoured vegetable stock
2 large carrots, finely diced
4 outer leaves Savoy cabbage or pak choi
    (bok choy), shredded
30ml/2 tbsp soy sauce
2.5ml/½ tsp sugar
2.5ml/½ tsp ground black pepper
fresh coriander (cilantro) leaves,
    to garnish

1 Put the egg in a bowl and beat lightly with a fork. Heat the oil in a small frying pan until it is hot, but not smoking. Pour in the egg and swirl the pan so that it coats the base evenly. Cook over a medium heat until the omelette has set and the underside is golden.

2 Slide the omelette out of the pan and roll it up like a pancake. Slice into 5mm/¼ in rounds and set aside for the garnish.

3 Put the stock into a large pan. Add the carrots and cabbage or pak choi and bring to the boil. Reduce the heat and simmer for 5 minutes, then add the soy sauce, sugar and pepper to season.

4 Stir well, then pour into warmed bowls. Lay a few omelette rounds on the surface of each portion and complete the garnish with the coriander leaves.

Nutritional information per portion: Energy 64kcal/264kJ; Protein 2.3g; Carbohydrate 4.3g, of which sugars 4.1g; Fat 4.3g, of which saturates 0.7g; Cholesterol 48mg; Calcium 27mg; Fibre 1.1g; Sodium 560mg.

Egg knot soup

Omelettes are often used to add protein to light Chinese soups like this one. In this recipe thin strips of omelette are tied into delicate knots, making this an attractive, as well as delicious, dish.

SERVES 4

1 spring onion (scallion), thinly shredded
800ml/1¹/₃ pints/3¹/₂ cups fish stock
5ml/1 tsp soy sauce
dash of rice wine or dry white wine
a pinch of salt

FOR THE PRAWN BALLS

200g/7oz/generous 1 cup large raw
   prawns (shrimp), shelled and deveined
65g/2¹/₂ oz cod fillet, skinned
5ml/1 tsp egg white
5ml/1 tsp rice wine, plus a dash extra
22.5ml/4¹/₂ tsp cornflour (cornstarch)
2–3 drops soy sauce
a pinch of salt

FOR THE OMELETTE

1 egg, beaten
a dash of rice wine
a pinch of salt
vegetable oil, for frying

1 To make the prawn balls, place all of the ingredients in a food processor and process to a thick, sticky paste. Shape the mixture into 4 balls, place in a steaming basket and steam over a pan of boiling water for 10 minutes.

2 To make the garnish, soak the spring onion in iced water for about 5 minutes, until the shreds curl, then drain.

3 To make the omelette, mix the egg with the mirin and salt. Heat a little oil in a frying pan and pour in the egg mixture, coating the pan evenly. When the omelette has set, turn it over and cook for 30 seconds. Leave to cool.

4 Cut the omelette into strips and tie each in a knot. Heat the stock or dashi, then add the soy sauce, sake or wine and salt. Divide the prawn balls and egg knots among four bowls and add the soup. Garnish with the spring onion.

Nutritional information per portion: Energy 98kcal/412kJ; Protein 13.6g; Carbohydrate 7.1g, of which sugars 0.2g; Fat 1.9g, of which saturates 0.5g; Cholesterol 153mg; Calcium 51mg; Fibre 0.1g; Sodium 218mg.

Chicken and crab noodle soup with coriander omelette

The chicken makes a delicious stock for this light noodle soup with its elusive hint of enticing aromatic Chinese flavours that are enhanced by delicate white crab meat.

SERVES 6

2 chicken legs, skinned
1.75 litres/3 pints/7$\frac{1}{2}$ cups water
bunch of spring onions (scallions)
2.5cm/1in piece fresh root ginger,
    finely sliced
5ml/1 tsp black peppercorns
2 garlic cloves, halved
75g/3oz rice noodles
115g/4oz fresh white crab meat

30ml/2 tbsp light soy sauce
salt and ground black pepper
coriander (cilantro) leaves, to garnish

FOR THE OMELETTES
4 eggs
30ml/2 tbsp chopped fresh
    coriander (cilantro) leaves
15ml/1 tbsp extra virgin olive oil

1 Put the chicken and water in a pan. Bring to the boil, reduce the heat and cook gently for 20 minutes; skim the surface occasionally.

2 Slice half the spring onions and add to the pan with the ginger, peppercorns, garlic and salt to taste. Cover and simmer for 1$\frac{1}{2}$ hours.

3 Meanwhile, soak the noodles in boiling water for 4 minutes, or according to the packet instructions. Drain and refresh under cold water. Shred the remaining spring onions and set aside.

4 To make the omelettes, beat the eggs with the coriander and seasoning. Heat a little of the olive oil in a small frying pan. Add a third of the egg and swirl the pan to coat the base evenly. Cook for 1 minute. Flip over and cook for 30 seconds. Turn the omelette out on to a plate and leave to cool. Repeat twice more to make three omelettes.

5 Roll up the omelettes tightly one at a time and slice thinly.

6 Remove the chicken from the stock and leave to cool. Strain the stock through a sieve (strainer) lined with muslin (cheesecloth) into a clean pan. When the chicken is cool enough to handle, remove and finely shred the meat, discarding the bones.

7 Bring the stock to the boil. Add the noodles, chicken, spring onions and crab meat, then simmer for 1–2 minutes. Stir in the soy sauce and season. Ladle the soup into bowls and top each with sliced omelette and coriander leaves.

Nutritional information per portion: Energy 159Kcal/664kJ; Protein 13.5g, Carbohydrate 10.6g, of which sugars 0.4g; Fat 6.9g, of which saturates 1.7g; Cholesterol 157mg; Calcium 46mg; Fibre 0g; Sodium 526mg.

Duck and preserved lime soup

This rich soup originates in the Chiu Chow region of southern China. This recipe can also be made with chicken stock and leftover duck meat from a roasted duck, or by roasting a duck, slicing off the breast portion and thigh meat for the soup.

SERVES 4–6

1 lean duck, about 1.5kg/3lb 5oz
2 preserved limes
25g/1oz fresh root ginger, thinly sliced
salt and ground black pepper

FOR THE GARNISH
vegetable oil, for frying
25g/1oz fresh root ginger, thinly sliced
    into strips
2 garlic cloves, thinly sliced into strips
2 spring onions (scallions), finely sliced

1 Place the duck in a large pan with enough water to cover. Season with salt and pepper and bring the water to the boil. Reduce the heat, cover the pan, and simmer for 1½ hours.

2 Add the preserved limes and ginger. Continue to simmer for another hour, skimming off the fat from time to time, until the liquid has reduced a little and the duck is so tender that it almost falls off the bone.

3 Heat some vegetable oil in a wok. Stir in the ginger and garlic and fry until golden. Drain them on kitchen paper and set aside for garnishing.

4 Remove the duck from the broth and shred the meat into individual bowls. Check the broth for seasoning, then ladle it over the duck in the bowls. Sprinkle the spring onions with the fried ginger and garlic over the top and serve.

Nutritional information per portion: Energy 124kcal/520kJ; Protein 19.8g; Carbohydrate 0.3g, of which sugars 0.3g; Fat 6.5g, of which saturates 1.3g; Cholesterol 110mg; Calcium 19mg; Fibre 0g; Sodium 110mg.

Duck and nut soup with jujubes

This thick soup is delicious. Packed with nuts and sweetened with jujubes (dried Chinese red dates), it resembles neither a soup nor a stew, but something in between. Served on its own, or with rice and pickles, it is a substantial meal in its own right.

SERVES 4

30–45ml/2–3 tbsp vegetable oil

4 duck legs, split into thighs
    and drumsticks

juice of 1 coconut

60ml/4 tbsp fish sauce

4 lemon grass stalks, bruised

12 chestnuts, peeled

90g/3¹/₂oz/scant 1 cup unsalted cashew
    nuts, roasted

90g/3¹/₂oz/scant 1 cup unsalted
    almonds, roasted

90g/3¹/₂oz/scant 1 cup unsalted
    peanuts, roasted

12 jujubes

salt and ground black pepper

a bunch of fresh basil leaves, to garnish

1 Heat the oil in a wok or heavy pan. Brown the duck legs in the oil and drain on kitchen paper.

2 Bring 2 litres/3¹/₂ pints/7³/₄ cups water to the boil. Reduce the heat and add the coconut juice, fish sauce, lemon grass and duck legs. Cover the pan and simmer over a gentle heat for 2–3 hours. Skim off any fat.

3 Add the nuts and jujubes and cook for 40 minutes, until the chestnuts are soft and the duck is very tender. Skim off any fat, season to taste and sprinkle with basil leaves to serve.

COOK'S TIP

To extract the coconut juice, pierce the eyes on top and turn the coconut upside down over a bowl.

Nutritional information per portion: Energy 604kcal/2512kJ; Protein 43.8g; Carbohydrate 8.9g, of which sugars 3.6g; Fat 44g, of which saturates 9.2g; Cholesterol 165mg; Calcium 49mg; Fibre 3.1g; Sodium 231mg.

Aromatic broth with roast duck

Served on its own, this Chinese soup makes a robust autumn or winter meal. In a Chinese household, a bowl of whole fresh or marinated chillies might be presented as a fiery side dish.

SERVES 4

15ml/1 tbsp vegetable oil
2 shallots, thinly sliced
4cm/1½in fresh root ginger, peeled and sliced
15ml/1 tbsp soy sauce
5ml/1 tsp five-spice powder
10ml/2 tsp sugar
175g/6oz pak choi (bok choy)
450g/1lb fresh egg noodles
350g/12oz roast duck, thinly sliced
sea salt
spring onions (scallions), and chopped coriander (cilantro) and basil, to garnish

FOR THE STOCK

1 duck carcass
2 carrots, peeled and quartered
2 onions, peeled and quartered
4cm/1½in fresh root ginger, peeled and cubed
2 lemon grass stalks, chopped
30ml/2 tbsp nuoc mam
15ml/1 tbsp soy sauce
6 black peppercorns

1 To make the stock, put the duck carcass into a deep pan. Add all the other stock ingredients and pour in 2.5 litres/4½ pints/10¼ cups water. Bring to the boil, and boil for a few minutes, skim off any foam, then reduce the heat and simmer gently with the lid on for 2–3 hours. Remove the lid and continue to simmer for a further 30 minutes to reduce the stock. Skim off any fat, season with salt, then strain the stock. Measure out 2 litres/3½ pints/8 cups.

2 Heat the oil in a wok or deep pan and stir in the shallots and ginger. Add the soy sauce, five-spice powder, sugar and stock and bring to the boil. Season with a little salt, reduce the heat and simmer for 10–15 minutes.

3 Cut the pak choi diagonally into wide strips and blanch in boiling water to soften. Drain and refresh under cold running water to prevent them from cooking any further. Bring a large pan of water to the boil, then add the noodles. Cook for 5 minutes, then drain.

4 Divide the noodles among four soup bowls, lay the strips of pak choi and duck over them, then ladle over the broth. Serve the soup garnished with spring onions, chillies and herbs.

Nutritional information per portion: Energy 673kcal/2836kJ; Protein 37g; Carbohydrate 86g, of which sugars 22g; Fat 6g, of which saturates 1g; Cholesterol 81mg; Calcium 4mg; Fibre 0.7g; Sodium 700mg.

Crispy wonton soup

The freshly cooked and crispy wontons are supposed to sizzle and 'sing' as the hot sesame oil hits the soup, so add them just before you take the bowls to the table.

SERVES 6

2 cloud ear (wood ear) mushrooms,
   soaked for 30 minutes in warm water
1.2 litres/2 pints/5 cups chicken stock
2.5cm/1in piece fresh root ginger, peeled
   and grated
4 spring onions (scallions), chopped
2 rich-green inner spring greens leaves,
   finely shredded
50g/2oz canned bamboo shoots, sliced
25ml/1½ tbsp dark soy sauce
2.5ml/½ tsp sesame oil
salt and ground black pepper

FOR THE FILLED WONTONS
5ml/1 tsp sesame oil
½ small onion, finely chopped
10 canned water chestnuts, drained
   and finely chopped
115g/4oz finely minced (ground) pork
24 wonton wrappers
groundnut (peanut) oil, for deep-frying

1 Make the filled wontons. Heat the sesame oil in a small pan, add the onion, water chestnuts and pork and fry, stirring occasionally, until the meat is no longer pink. Transfer to a bowl, season to taste and leave to cool.

2 Dampen the edges of a wonton wrapper. Place the other wrappers under a dampened dish towel so that they don't dry out. Place about 5ml/1 tsp of the filling in the centre of the wrapper. Gather it up like a purse and twist the top or roll up like a baby spring roll. Repeat for the remaining wontons.

3 To make the soup, drain the cloud ears, discarding the soaking liquid. Trim away any rough stems, then slice thinly. Bring the stock to the boil, add the ginger and spring onions and simmer for 3 minutes. Add the cloud ears, spring greens, bamboo shoots and soy sauce. Simmer for 10 minutes, then stir in the sesame oil, season with salt and pepper, cover and keep hot.

4 Heat the oil in a wok to 190°C/375°F and deep-fry the wontons for 3–4 minutes, until golden. Share among bowls of the soup and serve.

Nutritional information per portion: Energy 108kcal/456kJ; Protein 6.3g; Carbohydrate 14.4g, of which sugars 1.4g; Fat 3.3g, of which saturates 0.9g; Cholesterol 13mg; Calcium 69mg; Fibre 1.4g; Sodium 249mg.

Hot and sour soup

One of China's most popular soups, this is famed for its clever balance of flavours. The essential flavour contrast is provided by the 'hot' coming from pepper and the 'sour' from vinegar.

SERVES 4

4–6 dried Chinese mushrooms
115g/4oz pork fillet (tenderloin)
45ml/3 tbsp cornflour (cornstarch)
150ml/¼ pint/⅔ cup water
15–30ml/1–2 tbsp sunflower oil
1 small onion, finely chopped
1.5 litres/2½ pints/6¼ cups beef or
   chicken stock
150g/5oz fresh firm tofu, diced
60ml/4 tbsp rice vinegar
15ml/1 tbsp light soy sauce
1 egg, beaten
5 ml/1 tsp sesame oil
salt and ground white or
   black pepper
2–3 spring onions (scallions), shredded,
   to garnish

1 Place the dried mushrooms in a bowl, cover with warm water and soak for 30 minutes. Drain, reserving the soaking water. Cut off and discard the stems and slice the caps finely.

2 Cut the pork fillet into fine strips. Lightly dust the strips with some of the cornflour; mix the remaining cornflour with the water to form a smooth paste.

3 Heat the oil in a wok and fry the onion until soft, then add the pork and fry until it changes colour. Add the stock, mushrooms and soaking water then bring to the boil and simmer for 15 minutes. Lower the heat and stir in the cornflour paste to thicken. Add the tofu, vinegar, soy sauce, and salt and pepper.

4 Bring the soup to just below boiling point, then drizzle in the beaten egg by letting it drop from a whisk so that it forms threads in the soup. Stir in the sesame oil and serve at once, garnished with spring onion shreds.

Nutritional information per portion: Energy 103kcal/429kJ; Protein 7.3g; Carbohydrate 7.3g, of which sugars 0.3g; Fat 5.1g, of which saturates 1g; Cholesterol 44mg; Calcium 135mg; Fibre 0g; Sodium 208mg.

Liver with **matrimony vine soup**

Only the spinach-like leaves of the matrimony vine are eaten; the stems are discarded. Legend has it that if it is planted close to a house, marital discord will follow – hence the name 'matrimony vine'.

SERVES 4

200g/7oz pig's liver
4–6 stalks of matrimony vine
750ml/1¼ pints/3 cups fresh
   vegetable stock
30ml/2 tbsp fresh root ginger,
   finely shredded
30ml/2 tbsp light soy sauce
2.5ml/½ tsp ground black pepper
30ml/2 tbsp sesame oil

1 Put the liver in the freezer for about 10 minutes, until it is firm, then slice it very finely with a sharp knife.

2 Meanwhile, prepare the matrimony vine. Pull the leaves away from the stems, taking care to avoid the thorns. Wash the leaves thoroughly under plenty of cold running water and drain them in a colander.

3 Pour the stock into a large pan and bring to the boil. Add the ginger, soy sauce, pepper and sesame oil.

4 Add the matrimony vine leaves to the pan, simmer for 2 minutes, then add the sliced liver. Cook for 2 minutes more, until the liver is just cooked. Ladle the soup into warm bowls and serve immediately.

Nutritional information per portion: Energy 113kcal/472kJ; Protein 11.3g; Carbohydrate 0.9g, of which sugars 0.9g; Fat 7.2g, of which saturates 1.3g; Cholesterol 130mg; Calcium 31mg; Fibre 0.4g; Sodium 600mg.

Pork bone tea

Pork bone tea is a favourite at China's late-night hawker stalls. The broth is served with bowls of white rice, and the pieces of tender pork flesh are dipped into soy sauce infused with chillies.

SERVES 4–6

500g/1¼lb meaty pork ribs,
  trimmed and cut into 5cm/2in lengths
225g/8oz pork loin
8 garlic cloves, unpeeled and bruised
2 cinnamon sticks
5 star anise
120ml/4fl oz/½ cup light soy sauce
50ml/2fl oz/¼ cup dark soy sauce
15ml/1 tbsp sugar
salt and ground black pepper
steamed rice, to serve

FOR THE DIPPING SAUCE
120ml/4fl oz/½ cup light soy sauce
2 red chillies, seeded and finely chopped

FOR THE SPICE BAG
6 cloves
15ml/1 tbsp dried orange peel
5ml/1 tsp black peppercorns
5ml/1 tsp coriander seeds
5ml/1 tsp fennel seeds
a piece of muslin (cheesecloth)

1 To make the dipping sauce, stir the soy sauce and chillies together in a small bowl and set aside.

2 To make the spice bag, lay the piece of muslin flat and place all the spices in the centre. Gather up the edges and tie together to form a bag.

3 Put the pork ribs and loin into a deep pan. Add the garlic, cinnamon sticks, star anise and the spice bag. Pour in 2.5 litres/4½ pints/10 cups water and bring to the boil.

4 Skim off any fat from the surface, then stir in the soy sauces and sugar. Reduce the heat and simmer, partially covered, for about 2 hours, until the pork is almost falling off the bones. Season to taste with salt and lots of black pepper.

5 Remove the loin from the broth and cut it into bitesize pieces. Remove the spice bag and discard. Divide the meat and ribs among four to six bowls and ladle the broth over the meat. Remove the star anise and cinnamon, or retain them for decoration only.

6 Serve with the soy and chilli sauce as a dip for the pieces of pork, and steamed rice. Guests will need a fork or chopsticks to eat and dip the pieces of meat and a spoon for the broth.

Nutritional information per portion: Energy 49kcal/206kJ; Protein 8.1g; Carbohydrate 0.8g, of which sugars 0.8g; Fat 1.5g, of which saturates 0.5g; Cholesterol 24mg; Calcium 3mg; Fibre 0g; Sodium 145mg.

Chinese cabbage, meatball and noodle broth

This wonderfully fragrant combination of spiced meatballs, noodles and vegetables cooked slowly in a richly flavoured broth makes for a very hearty, warming soup. Serve it as a main course on a cold winter evening, drizzled with chilli oil for a little extra heat.

SERVES 4

10 dried shiitake mushrooms

90g/3¹/₂oz bean thread noodles

675g/1¹/₂lb minced (ground) beef

10ml/2 tsp finely grated garlic

10ml/2 tsp finely grated fresh root ginger

1 red chilli, seeded and chopped

6 spring onions (scallions), finely sliced

1 egg white

15ml/1 tbsp cornflour (cornstarch)

15ml/1 tbsp rice wine

30ml/2 tbsp sunflower oil

1.5 litres/2¹/₂ pints/6¹/₄ cups chicken
   or beef stock

50ml/2fl oz/¹/₄ cup light soy sauce

5ml/1 tsp sugar

150g/5oz enoki mushrooms, trimmed

200g/7oz Chinese leaves (Chinese cabbage), very thinly sliced

salt and ground black pepper

sesame oil and chilli oil,
   to drizzle (optional)

1 Place the dried mushrooms in a bowl and pour over 250ml/8fl oz/1 cup boiling water. Leave to soak for 30 minutes and then squeeze dry, reserving the soaking liquid.

2 Cut the stems from the mushrooms and discard, then thickly slice the caps and set aside.

3 Put the noodles in a large bowl and pour over boiling water to cover. Leave to soak for 3–4 minutes, then drain, rinse and set aside.

4 Place the beef, garlic, ginger, chilli, spring onions, egg white, cornflour, rice wine and seasoning in a food processor. Process to combine well.

5 Transfer the mixture to a bowl and divide into 30 portions, then shape each one into a ball.

6 Heat a wok over a high heat and add the oil. Fry the meatballs, in batches, for 2–3 minutes on each side until lightly browned. Remove with a slotted spoon and drain on kitchen paper.

7 Wipe out the wok and place over a high heat. Add the stock, soy sauce, sugar and shiitake mushrooms with the reserved soaking liquid and bring to the boil.

8 Add the meatballs to the boiling stock, reduce the heat and cook gently for 20–25 minutes.

9 Add the noodles, enoki mushrooms and Chinese leaves to the wok and cook gently for 4–5 minutes. Serve ladled into wide shallow bowls. Drizzle with sesame oil and chilli oil.

Nutritional information per portion: Energy 548kcal/2279kJ; Protein 36.8g; Carbohydrate 24.9g, of which sugars 3g; Fat 33.3g, of which saturates 12.4g; Cholesterol 101mg; Calcium 52mg; Fibre 1.7g; Sodium 161mg.

Beef noodle soup

A steaming and substantial bowl of this Chinese classic, packed with delicious flavours and a true taste of the Orient, will be especially welcome on cold winter days.

SERVES 4

10g/¹/₄oz dried Chinese mushrooms
150 ml/¹/₄ pint/²/₃ cup boiling water
6 spring onions (scallions)
115g/4oz carrots
350g/12oz rump (round) steak
about 30ml/2 tbsp sunflower oil
1 garlic clove, crushed
2.5cm/1in piece fresh root ginger, peeled
   and finely chopped
1.2 litres/2 pints/5 cups beef stock
45ml/3 tbsp light soy sauce
60ml/4 tbsp rice wine
75g/3oz thin egg noodles
75g/3oz spinach, shredded
salt and ground black pepper

1 Break the mushrooms into small pieces, place in a bowl and pour over the boiling water. Set aside to soak for 15 minutes. Shred the spring onions and carrots into 5cm/2in-long fine strips. Slice the rump steak into thin strips.

2 Heat the oil in a pan and cook the beef in batches until browned. Remove the beef and set aside to drain on kitchen paper. Add the garlic, ginger, spring onions and carrots to the pan and stir-fry for 3 minutes.

3 Add the stock, the mushrooms and their soaking liquid, the soy sauce, rice wine and then season. Bring to the boil and simmer, covered, for 10 minutes.

4 Break up the noodles slightly and add to the pan, with the spinach. Simmer for 5 minutes and then serve.

Nutritional information per portion: Energy 124kcal/520kJ; Protein 19.8g; Carbohydrate 0.3g, of which sugars 0.3g; Fat 6.5g, of which saturates 1.3g; Cholesterol 110mg; Calcium 19mg; Fibre 0g; Sodium 110mg.

Bamboo shoot, fish and rice soup

This is a refreshing dish made with freshwater fish such as carp or catfish. The addition of rice to the fragrant broth makes this a rewarding and substantial main course soup.

SERVES 4

2.5 litres/4¹/₄ pints/10 cups fish stock
45ml/3 tbsp fish sauce
15ml/1 tbsp soy sauce
75g/3oz/scant ¹/₂ cup long grain rice
250ml/8fl oz/1 cup coconut milk
2 lemon grass stalks, trimmed and crushed
25g/1oz galangal, thinly sliced
2–3 red chillies
4 garlic cloves, crushed
15ml/1 tbsp palm sugar (jaggery)
1 fresh bamboo shoot, peeled, boiled in
   water for 10 minutes, and sliced
450g/1lb freshwater fish fillets, skinned
   and cut into bitesize pieces
a small bunch of fresh basil leaves
a small bunch of fresh coriander (cilantro),
   chopped, and 1 chilli, sliced, to garnish

1 Put the stock into a large pan with the fish and soy sauce and bring it to the boil. Stir in the rice and reduce the heat to a simmer.

2 Add the coconut milk, lemon grass, galangal, chillies, garlic and sugar to the pan. Simmer for about 10 minutes to let the flavours mingle. The rice should be just cooked, with bite to it.

3 Add the sliced bamboo shoot and the pieces of fish. Simmer for 5 minutes, until the fish is cooked. Check the seasoning and stir in the basil leaves.

4 Ladle the soup into warmed soup bowls and garnish with the chopped coriander and sliced chilli. Serve immediately.

Nutritional information per portion: Energy 269kcal/1130kJ; Protein 35.5g; Carbohydrate 23.2g, of which sugars 7.9g; Fat 3.8g, of which saturates 1.1g; Cholesterol 87mg; Calcium 109mg; Fibre 2.6g; Sodium 214mg.

Chinese fish ball soup

This traditional soup is often eaten as a snack or light lunch, garnished with spring onions and fresh chillies, and the Chinese often add an extra kick with a drizzle of chilli oil.

SERVES 4–6

450g/1lb fresh fish fillets (such as haddock, cod, whiting or bream), boned and flaked
15–30ml/1–2 tbsp rice flour
salt and ground black pepper

FOR THE SOUP
1.5 litres/2¹/₂ pints/6¹/₄ cups fish stock
15–30ml/1–2 tbsp light soy sauce
4–6 mustard green leaves, shredded
90g/3¹/₂oz mung bean thread noodles, soaked in hot water until soft
2 finely sliced spring onions (scallions), 1 sliced red chilli, and fresh coriander (cilantro) leaves, to garnish

1 To make the fish balls, grind the flaked flesh to a paste, using a mortar and pestle or food processor. Season with salt and pepper and stir in 60ml/4 tbsp water. Add enough rice flour to form a paste. Take small portions of fish paste into your hands and mould them into balls.

2 Meanwhile, bring the stock to the boil in a deep pan and season to taste with soy sauce.

3 Drop the fish balls into the stock. Bring the stock back to the boil, then lower the heat and simmer for 5 minutes. Add the mustard greens and cook for 1 minute until tender.

4 Divide the noodles among four to six bowls. Using a slotted spoon, add the fish balls and greens, then ladle over the hot stock. Garnish with the spring onions and chilli and sprinkle the chopped coriander over the top.

Nutritional information per portion: Energy 127kcal/533kJ; Protein 14.9g; Carbohydrate 14.8g, of which sugars 0.5g; Fat 0.6g, of which saturates 0.1g; Cholesterol 35mg; Calcium 17mg; Fibre 0.2g; Sodium 408mg.

Hokkein prawn noodle soup

Hailing from the Chinese province of Fujian, Hokkein noodle soup is an enduringly popular dish. Traditionally, it is served with cubes of pork fat, but in this recipe crispy bacon has been used instead.

SERVES 4–6

45ml/3 tbsp dried shrimp
1 dried red chilli
50g/2oz root ginger, peeled and sliced
2 onions, quartered
4 garlic cloves, bruised
2 lemon grass stalks, bruised
2.5ml/¹/₂ tsp black peppercorns
30–45ml/2–3 tbsp dark soy sauce
700g/1lb 10oz pork and chicken bones

FOR THE STOCK
15ml/1 tbsp sugar
6 rashers (strips) streaky
    (fatty) bacon
150g/5oz fresh egg noodles
20 fresh, large prawns (shrimp), peeled
    (add the shells to the stock)
90g/3¹/₂oz beansprouts
2 spring onions (scallions), trimmed and
    finely sliced
salt and ground black pepper

1 Put all the stock ingredients into a deep pan along with the prawn shells. Pour in 2 litres/3¹/₂ pints/7³/₄ cups water and bring to the boil. Reduce the heat and simmer gently, uncovered, for about 2 hours, until the stock has reduced by half.

2 Strain the stock into a clean pan and put it over a low heat to keep hot. Season with salt and pepper to taste.

3 In a small pan, heat the sugar with 15ml/1 tbsp water. Stir over a low heat until the sugar dissolves, then boil without stirring until it turns a rich brown. Mix it into the stock.

4 Cut the bacon into 1cm/¹/₂in slices. In a heavy pan, dry-fry the bacon until it turns crispy and golden. Drain on kitchen paper and set aside.

5 Using a perforated ladle or sieve (strainer), plunge the noodles into the hot stock for 1 minute to heat through, then divide them among bowls. Add the prawns to the stock, heat for 1 minute, remove with a slotted spoon and add to the bowls. Add the beansprouts to the prawns and noodles and ladle the hot stock into the bowls. Sprinkle the crispy bacon and spring onions over the top and serve immediately.

Nutritional information per portion: Energy 257kcal/1082kJ; Protein 18.7g; Carbohydrate 27.1g, of which sugars 6.9g; Fat 9g, of which saturates 2.8g; Cholesterol 94mg; Calcium 145mg; Fibre 3g; Sodium 1080mg.

Seafood wonton soup

This is a variation on the popular wonton soup that is traditionally prepared using pork. In this version the fat content is reduced by substituting prawns, scallops and cod.

SERVES 4

50g/2oz raw tiger prawns (jumbo shrimp)
50g/2oz queen scallops
75g/3oz skinless cod fillet, roughly chopped
15ml/1 tbsp finely chopped chives
5ml/1 tsp dry sherry
1 small (US medium) egg white, lightly beaten
2.5ml/1/2 tsp sesame oil

1.5ml/1/4 tsp salt
a large pinch of ground white pepper
20 wonton wrappers
900ml/1 1/2 pints/3 3/4 cups fish stock
2 cos lettuce leaves, shredded
fresh coriander (cilantro) leaves and garlic chives,
    to garnish

1 Peel the prawns, then devein them using the point of a sharp knife. Rinse them well, pat them dry on kitchen paper and cut them into small pieces.

2 Rinse the scallops in a sieve (strainer) under cold water. Pat them dry, using kitchen paper. Chop them into small pieces so that they are the same size as the prawns.

3 Place the cod in a food processor and process until a smooth paste is formed. Scrape the paste into a bowl and stir in the prawns, scallops, chives, sherry, egg white, sesame oil, salt and pepper.

4 Mix all of the ingredients thoroughly, cover with clear film (plastic wrap) and leave in a cool place to marinate for at least 20 minutes.

5 Make the wontons. Place a teaspoonful of the seafood filling in the centre of a wonton wrapper, then bring the corners together to meet at the top.

6 Twist the edges of the wonton together to completely enclose the filling. Fill the remaining wonton wrappers in the same way.

7 Pour the fish stock into a pan and heat it gently over low heat. Do not let it boil, but ensure that it is piping hot.

8 Bring a large pan of water to the boil. Add the wontons to the pan using a spoon. When the water returns to the boil, lower the heat and simmer the wontons gently for 5 minutes or until they float to the surface. Drain the wontons and divide them among four heated soup bowls.

9 Add a portion of shredded lettuce to each bowl. Ladle the hot fish stock into each bowl, garnish each portion with coriander leaves and garlic chives and serve immediately.

Nutritional information per portion: Energy 113kcal/478kJ; Protein 11.3g; Carbohydrate 15.7g, of which sugars 0.9g; Fat 0.8g, of which saturates 0.2g; Cholesterol 39mg; Calcium 53mg; Fibre 0.9g; Sodium 75mg.

Appetizers & dim sum

Deliciously moreish dim sum and elegant appetizers are the heart of a true Chinese feast. This chapter features mouthwatering and authentic recipes, such as temptingly fragrant Steamed Pork Buns and traditional Radish Cake, as well as showstopping dinner party dishes, including Wenchang Steamed Crab, and Clams with Chilli in Yellow Bean Sauce.

Deep-fried tofu sheets stuffed with spiced vegetables

Tofu sheets are made from soya milk. The milk is boiled and the skin that forms on the top is then lifted off and dried in sheets. They are available in Asian supermarkets and need to be soaked briefly in water before filling and frying until deliciously crisp and golden.

SERVES 4

30ml/2 tbsp groundnut (peanut) oil

50g/2oz fresh enoki mushrooms, finely chopped

1 garlic clove, crushed

4 spring onions (scallions), finely shredded

1 small carrot, cut into thin matchsticks

115g/4oz bamboo shoots, cut into thin matchsticks

5ml/1 tsp grated fresh root ginger

15ml/1 tbsp light soy sauce

5ml/1 tsp chilli sauce

5ml/1 tsp sugar

15ml/1 tbsp cornflour (cornstarch)

8 tofu sheets (approximately 18 x 22cm/7 x 9in each)

sunflower oil, for frying

crisp salad leaves, to serve

1 Heat the groundnut oil in a wok over a high heat and add the chopped mushrooms, garlic, spring onions, carrot, bamboo shoots and ginger. Stir-fry for 2–3 minutes, then add the soy sauce, chilli sauce and sugar and toss to mix thoroughly.

2 Remove the vegetables from the wok and place in a sieve (strainer) to drain any excess juices. Set them aside to cool.

3 In a small bowl, mix the cornflour with 60ml/4 tbsp cold water to form a smooth paste. Soak the bean curd sheets in a bowl of warm water for 10–15 seconds and then lay them out on a clean work surface and pat dry with kitchen paper.

4 Brush the edges of one of the tofu sheets with the cornflour paste and place 30–45ml/2–3 tbsp of the vegetable mixture at one end of the sheet. Fold the edges over toward the centre and roll up tightly to form a neat roll. Repeat with the remaining tofu sheets and filling.

5 Place the rolls on a baking parchment-lined baking sheet or tray, cover and chill for 3–4 hours.

6 To cook, fill a wok one-third full with sunflower oil and heat to 180°C/350°F (or until a cube of bread, dropped into the oil, browns in 45 seconds).

7 Working in batches, deep-fry the rolls for 2–3 minutes, or until crisp and golden. Drain on kitchen paper and serve immediately with crisp salad leaves.

Nutritional information per portion: Energy 288kcal/1190kJ; Protein 9.5g; Carbohydrate 3.2g, of which sugars 2.2g; Fat 26.5g, of which saturates 3.2g; Cholesterol 0mg; Calcium 524mg; Fibre 1g; Sodium 10mg.

Chilli and pak choi omelette parcels

Colourful stir-fried vegetables and coriander in black bean sauce make a remarkably good omelette filling, which is quick and easy to prepare.

SERVES 4

130g/4¹/₂oz broccoli, cut into
    small florets
30ml/2 tbsp groundnut (peanut) oil
1cm/¹/₂in piece fresh root ginger, finely
    grated
1 large garlic clove, crushed
2 fresh red chillies, seeded and
    finely sliced
4 spring onions (scallions),
    diagonally sliced
175g/6oz/3 cups pak choi
    (bok choy), shredded
50g/2oz/2 cups fresh coriander (cilantro)
    leaves, plus extra to garnish
115g/4oz/2 cups beansprouts
45ml/3 tbsp black bean sauce
4 eggs
salt and ground black pepper

1 Bring a pan of salted water to the boil and blanch the broccoli for 2 minutes. Drain, then refresh under cold running water, and drain again.

2 Heat 15ml/1 tbsp of the oil in a frying pan and stir-fry the ginger, garlic and half the chillies for 1 minute. Add the spring onions, broccoli and pak choi, and toss over the heat for 2 minutes more.

3 Chop half of the coriander and add to the pan. Add the beansprouts and stir-fry for 1 minute, then add the black bean sauce and heat through for 1 minute more. Keep warm.

4 Mix the eggs lightly in a bowl with a fork and season well. Heat a little of the oil in a small frying pan and add one-quarter of the beaten egg. Tilt the pan so that the egg covers the base, then sprinkle over one-quarter of the reserved coriander leaves. Cook the egg until set, then turn out the omelette on to a plate and keep warm while you make 3 more omelettes.

5 Spoon one-quarter of the stir-fry on to each omelette and roll up. Cut in half crossways and serve, garnished with the remaining coriander leaves and chilli slices.

Nutritional information per portion: Energy 148kcal/614kJ; Protein 10.4g; Carbohydrate 6.2g, of which sugars 5.4g; Fat 9.3g, of which saturates 2.2g; Cholesterol 190mg; Calcium 152mg; Fibre 3g; Sodium 323mg.

Lettuce parcels

This is a popular 'assemble-it-yourself' treat in Hong Kong. The filling – a blend of textures and flavours – is served with lettuce leaves, which are spread with hoisin sauce and used as wrappers.

SERVES 6

2 boneless chicken breast portions, total
    weight about 350g/12oz
4 dried Chinese mushrooms,
    soaked for 30 minutes in warm
    water to cover
30ml/2 tbsp vegetable oil
2 garlic cloves, crushed
6 drained canned water chestnuts,
    thinly sliced
30ml/2 tbsp light soy sauce
5ml/1 tsp Sichuan peppercorns,
    dry-fried and crushed
4 spring onions (scallions),
    finely chopped
5ml/1 tsp sesame oil
vegetable oil, for deep-frying
50g/2oz cellophane noodles
salt and ground black pepper
    (optional)
1 crisp lettuce and 60ml/4 tbsp hoisin
    sauce, to serve

1 Remove the skin from the chicken breasts, pat the skin dry and set aside. Chop the chicken into thin strips. Drain the soaked Chinese mushrooms. Cut off and discard the mushroom stems; slice the caps finely and set aside.

2 Heat the oil in a wok. Add the garlic, then add the chicken and stir-fry until the pieces are cooked through and no longer pink. Add the sliced mushrooms, water chestnuts, soy sauce and peppercorns. Toss for 2–3 minutes, then season, if needed. Stir in half of the spring onions, then the sesame oil. Remove from the heat and keep warm.

3 Heat the oil for deep-frying to 190°C/375°F. Cut the chicken skin into strips, deep-fry until very crisp then drain on kitchen paper. Add the noodles to the hot oil and deep-fry until crisp. Drain on kitchen paper.

4 Crush the noodles and put in a serving dish. Top with the chicken skin, chicken mixture and remaining spring onions. Toss to mix. Arrange the lettuce leaves on a platter.

5 Guests can take one or two lettuce leaves, spread the inside with hoisin sauce and add a spoonful of filling, rolling them into a parcel.

Nutritional information per portion: Energy 195kcal/821kJ; Protein 28.7g; Carbohydrate 7.5g, of which sugars 0.6g; Fat 5.5g, of which saturates 0.9g; Cholesterol 82mg; Calcium 11mg; Fibre 0.1g; Sodium 428mg.

Fragrant rice paper parcels
with **wilted choi sum**

Translucent rice paper makes a wonderfully crisp wrapping for this vegetable and tofu filling that is lightly spiced with the flavours of coriander and warming chilli. Take care when handling the papers because they are very brittle and can easily be damaged.

SERVES 4

30ml/2 tbsp sunflower oil

90g/3¹/₂oz shiitake mushrooms, stalks
   discarded and finely chopped

30ml/2 tbsp chopped garlic

90g/3¹/₂oz water chestnuts, finely chopped

90g/3¹/₂oz firm tofu, finely chopped

2 spring onions (scallions), finely chopped

¹/₂ red (bell) pepper, seeded and
   finely chopped

50g/2oz mangetouts (snow peas),
   finely chopped

15ml/1 tbsp light soy sauce

15ml/1 tbsp sweet chilli sauce

45ml/3 tbsp chopped fresh coriander
   (cilantro)

30ml/2 tbsp chopped fresh mint leaves

90ml/6 tbsp plain (all-purpose) flour

12 medium rice paper wrappers

sunflower oil, for frying

500g/1¹/₄lb choi sum or Chinese greens, roughly
   sliced or chopped

egg fried rice, to serve

1 Heat the oil in a wok over a high heat and add the chopped mushrooms. Stir-fry for 3 minutes and then add the garlic and stir-fry for a further 1 minute.

2 Add the water chestnuts, tofu, spring onions, red pepper and mangetouts to the wok. Stir-fry for 2–3 minutes and then add the soy and sweet chilli sauces. Remove from the heat and stir in the chopped coriander and mint. Leave to cool completely.

3 Place the flour in a bowl and stir in 105ml/7 tbsp cold water to make a thick, smooth paste.

4 Fill a large bowl with warm water and dip a rice paper wrapper in it for a few minutes until softened. Remove and drain on a dish towel.

5 Divide the filling into 12 portions and spoon one portion on to the softened rice wrapper. Fold in each side and roll up tightly. Seal the ends with a little of the flour paste. Repeat with the remaining wrappers and filling.

6 Fill a wok one-third full with the oil and heat to 180°C/350°F (or until a cube of bread, dropped into the oil, browns in 15 seconds). Working in batches of 2–3, deep-fry the parcels for 3 minutes until crisp and lightly browned. Drain well on kitchen paper and keep warm.

7 Pour off most of the oil, reserving 30ml/2 tbsp. Place over a medium heat and add the choi sum. Stir-fry for 3–4 minutes. Divide among four warmed bowls and top with the parcels. Serve immediately with egg fried rice.

Nutritional information per portion: Energy 252kcal/1051kJ; Protein 10.2g; Carbohydrate 34.6g, of which sugars 6.6g; Fat 8.5g, of which saturates 1g; Cholesterol 0mg; Calcium 448mg; Fibre 6.8g; Sodium 313mg.

Crystal dumplings

These dumplings are called chui kuay (water dumplings) in China on account of their translucent skins. They are especially delicious with a sweet soy sauce and chilli dip.

SERVES 6–8

200g/7oz/1³/₄ cups sweet potato flour
400ml/14fl oz/1²/₃ cups water
30ml/2 tbsp vegetable oil
115g/4oz/1 cup tapioca flour

FOR THE FILLING
400g/14oz can bamboo shoots,
    drained
45ml/3 tbsp vegetable oil
3 garlic cloves, crushed
30ml/2 tbsp dark soy sauce

30ml/2 tbsp oyster sauce
5ml/1 tsp ground black pepper
200ml/7fl oz/scant 1 cup water

SWEET SOY SAUCE AND CHILLI DIP
45ml/3 tbsp dark soy sauce
15ml/1 tbsp ginger purée
15ml/1 tbsp rice vinegar
15ml/1 tbsp sesame oil
5ml/1 tsp sugar
5ml/1 tsp chilli bean paste

1 Put the sweet potato flour in a pan. Blend in the water and oil and cook a over low heat, stirring occasionally, until thick. Leave to cool for 15 minutes.

2 Shred the bamboo shoots for the filling until they are more or less the shape and size of beansprouts. Rinse thoroughly and drain.

3 Heat the oil in a wok and fry the garlic over a low heat for 40 seconds. Add the bamboo shoots, soy sauce, oyster sauce, pepper and water. Cook over a medium heat for 10 minutes, until almost dry. Set aside to cool.

4 Stir the tapioca flour into the sweet potato flour mixture. Mix, then transfer to a floured board and knead for 5 minutes. Shape the dough into a long roll, about 5cm/2in in diameter. Slice off pieces 9mm/³/₈in thick and flatten each with a rolling pin to form very thin, unbroken circles.

5 Place 30ml/2 tbsp bamboo shoots on each circle, fold over into a half-moon shape and seal the edges. Pinch until you get a serrated edge on each dumpling. Place the dumplings on an oiled plate and steam over a wok of rapidly boiling water for 30 minutes, topping up the water as necessary.

6 Mix together all the ingredients for the sweet soy sauce and chilli dip in a small bowl. Transfer to a serving bowl. Serve the dumplings warm with the dip.

Nutritional information per portion: Energy 244kcal/1022kJ; Protein 3.6g; Carbohydrate 38.2g, of which sugars 5.2g; Fat 8.7g, of which saturates 1.1g; Cholesterol 0mg; Calcium 21mg; Fibre 1.3g; Sodium 1134mg.

Shanghai tofu spring rolls

It is said that these crisp snacks were traditionally served with tea when visitors came to call after the Chinese New Year. As this was springtime, they came to be known as spring rolls.

MAKES 12

12 spring roll wrappers, thawed if frozen
30ml/2 tbsp plain (all-purpose) flour,
    mixed to a paste with water
sunflower oil, for deep-frying

FOR THE FILLING
6 dried Chinese mushrooms, soaked for
    30 minutes in warm water
150g/5oz fresh firm tofu
30ml/2 tbsp sunflower oil
225g/8oz finely minced (ground) pork
225g/8oz peeled cooked prawns
    (shrimp), coarsely chopped
2.5ml/1/2 tsp cornflour (cornstarch),
    mixed to a paste with 15ml/1 tbsp
    light soy sauce
75g/3oz each shredded bamboo shoots,
    sliced water chestnuts and beansprouts
6 spring onions (scallions), finely chopped
a little sesame oil

1 To make the filling, drain the mushrooms. Cut off and discard the stems and slice the caps finely. Slice the tofu. Heat the oil in a wok and stir-fry the pork for 2–3 minutes, until the colour changes. Add the prawns, cornflour paste and bamboo shoots. Stir in the water chestnuts.

2 Increase the heat, add the beansprouts and spring onions and toss for 1 minute. Stir in the mushrooms and tofu. Remove the wok from the heat, then stir in the sesame oil. Cool quickly on a large platter.

3 Place a spring roll wrapper on the work surface with one corner nearest you. Spoon some of the filling near the centre of the wrapper and fold the nearest corner over the filling. Brush a little of the flour paste on the free sides, turn the sides into the middle and roll up to enclose the filling. Repeat with the remaining wrappers and filling.

4 Deep-fry the spring rolls, in batches, in oil heated to 190°C/375°F until they are golden. Drain and serve immediately with sweet chilli dipping sauce.

Nutritional information per portion: Energy 108kcal/456kJ; Protein 6.3g; Carbohydrate 14.4g, of which sugars 1.4g; Fat 3.3g, of which saturates 0.9g; Cholesterol 13mg; Calcium 69mg; Fibre 1.4g; Sodium 249mg.

Mini spring rolls

Eat these delightfully light and crispy parcels with your fingers. If you relish slightly spicier food, sprinkle them with a little cayenne pepper before serving.

MAKES 20

75g/3oz cooked chicken breast
120ml/4fl oz/½ cup vegetable oil
1 small onion, finely chopped
1 clove garlic, crushed
1 green chilli, seeded and
    finely chopped
1 small carrot, cut into
    fine matchsticks
1 spring onion (scallion), finely sliced
1 small red (bell) pepper, seeded and cut
    into fine matchsticks
25g/1oz beansprouts
5ml/1 tsp sesame oil
4 large sheets filo pastry
1 egg white, lightly beaten
fresh chives, to garnish
    (optional)
light soy sauce, to serve

1 Using a sharp knife, slice the chicken breast into thin strips. Heat a wok, then add 30ml/2 tbsp of the vegetable oil. When it is hot, add the onion, garlic and chilli and stir-fry for 1 minute. Add the chicken strips to the wok and fry over a high heat, stirring constantly until they are browned all over.

2 Add the carrot, spring onion and red pepper to the wok and stir-fry for 2 minutes. Add the beansprouts, stir in the sesame oil, then remove the wok from the heat and leave the mixture to cool.

3 Cut each sheet of filo pastry into five short strips. Place a small amount of the filling at one end of each strip, leaving a small border at the edges, then fold in the long sides and roll up the pastry. Seal and glaze the parcels with the egg white, then chill them, uncovered, for 15 minutes before frying.

4 Wipe out the wok with kitchen paper, reheat it, and add the remaining oil. When the oil is hot, add the rolls in batches and stir-fry until they are golden. Drain and serve garnished with chives and with light soy sauce for dipping.

Nutritional information per portion: Energy 72kcal/300kJ; Protein 1.9g; Carbohydrate 5.4g, of which sugars 0.5g; Fat 4.9g, of which saturates 1.1g; Cholesterol 2.2mg; Calcium 10mg; Fibre 0.6g; Sodium 144mg.

Chive dumplings

These dumplings are lovely and light, thanks to the wheat starch flour used for the wrappers. Although there is an art to making them, the end result is well worth the effort. The Chinese chives used in this recipe are flatter and broader than regular chives, with a distinctive, fresh aroma.

SERVES 6–8

150g/5oz/1¼ cups wheat starch
200ml/7fl oz/scant 1 cup water
15ml/1 tbsp vegetable oil
50g/2oz/½ cup tapioca flour
a pinch of salt
sesame oil, for brushing the dumplings
chilli sauce, for dipping

FOR THE FILLING
200g/7oz Chinese chives
30ml/2 tbsp light soy sauce
15ml/1 tbsp sesame oil
2.5ml/½ tsp ground black pepper
15ml/1 tbsp cornflour (cornstarch)
1 egg, lightly beaten

1 Put the wheat starch in a non-stick pan. Mix in the water and oil and cook over a low heat, stirring occasionally, until very thick. Remove from the heat and leave to cool for 15 minutes.

2 Meanwhile, prepare the filling. Chop the chives finely. Put them in a bowl and stir in the soy sauce, sesame oil, pepper and cornflour. Heat a wok, add the mixture and toss over low heat for 5 minutes. Stir in the lightly beaten egg to bind the mixture, then set it aside.

3 Stir the tapioca flour and salt into the cool wheat starch mixture. Mix well, then transfer to a floured board. Knead for at least 5 minutes. Roll out the dough and stamp out into 12 circles, 7.5cm/3in in diameter.

4 Place 1 heaped tablespoon of the filling on each dough circle and fold to make half-moon shapes. Seal the edges with a little water. Brush each dumpling with a little sesame oil to prevent them from sticking together when being steamed.

5 Place the dumplings on a plate and steam over rapidly boiling water for 10 minutes. Serve immediately, with a chilli sauce dip.

Nutritional information per portion: Energy 140kcal/589kJ; Protein 1.8g; Carbohydrate 25.9g, of which sugars 0.9g; Fat 3.9g, of which saturates 0.6g; Cholesterol 24mg; Calcium 58mg; Fibre 1.3g; Sodium 295mg.

Spiced noodle pancakes

The delicate rice noodles puff up in the hot oil to give a wonderfully crunchy bite that melts in the mouth. For maximum enjoyment, serve the golden pancakes as soon as they are cooked and savour the subtle blend of spices and wonderfully crisp texture.

SERVES 4

150g/5oz dried thin rice noodles
1 red chilli, finely diced
10ml/2 tsp garlic salt
5ml/1 tsp ground ginger
¼ small red onion,
    very finely diced
5ml/1 tsp finely chopped
    lemon grass
5ml/1 tsp ground cumin
5ml/1 tsp ground coriander
a large pinch of ground turmeric
salt
vegetable oil, for frying
sweet chilli sauce, for dipping

1 Roughly break up the noodles and place in a large bowl. Pour over enough boiling water to cover and soak for 4–5 minutes. Drain and rinse under cold water. Dry on kitchen paper.

2 Transfer the noodles to a bowl and add the chilli, garlic salt, ground ginger, red onion, lemon grass, ground cumin, coriander and turmeric. Toss well to mix and season with salt.

3 Heat 5–6cm/2–2½in oil in a wok. Working in batches, drop tablespoons of the noodle mixture into the oil. Flatten using the back of a skimmer and cook for 1–2 minutes on each side until crisp and golden. Drain on kitchen paper and serve with the chilli sauce.

Nutritional information per portion: Energy 190kcal/791kJ; Protein 2g; Carbohydrate 31.8g, of which sugars 0.9g; Fat 5.6g, of which saturates 0.7g; Cholesterol 0mg; Calcium 9mg; Fibre 0.2g; Sodium 496mg.

Radish cake

This recipe makes innovative use of the large white radish that is also known as mooli or daikon. As a vegetable, white radish is fairly bland, although it is useful for making soup stock. Process it to a paste and mix it with rice flour, however, and it is magically transformed.

SERVES 6–8

50g/2oz dried shrimp

1kg/2¹/₄lb white radish, (mooli or daikon)

300g/11oz/2 cups rice flour

115g/4oz/1 cup tapioca flour or 115g/4oz/1 cup cornflour (cornstarch)

750ml/1¹/₄ pints/3 cups water

5ml/1 tsp salt

30ml/2 tbsp vegetable oil

30ml/2 tbsp light soy sauce

30ml/2 tbsp sesame oil

2.5ml/¹/₂ tsp ground black pepper

dipping sauce (optional), to serve

1 Soak the dried shrimp in a bowl of water for 1 hour, until soft. Meanwhile, peel the radish and chop it roughly. Process it in batches in a food processor to a soft white purée. Scrape into a sieve (strainer) and press down with a spoon to extract as much liquid as possible. Put the radish purée into a bowl and stir in the rice flour and the tapioca or cornflour. Add the water and salt. Mix well.

2 Drain the soaked shrimp and chop them roughly. Spoon the radish purée into a non-stick pan and cook over a low heat, stirring frequently, for 5 minutes.

3 Heat the vegetable oil in a frying pan or wok. Add the chopped shrimp and fry for 2 minutes, then add the radish purée. Stir well, then add the soy sauce, sesame oil and black pepper. Mix thoroughly to combine.

4 Press the mixture into a lightly oiled steaming tray. Steam over a pan of boiling water for 20 minutes. Set aside. When cold, slice into bitesize pieces and serve plain or with a dipping sauce of your choice.

Nutritional information per portion: Energy 263kcal/1099kJ; Protein 7g; Carbohydrate 44.2g, of which sugars 2.7g; Fat 6.3g, of which saturates 0.9g; Cholesterol 32mg; Calcium 111mg; Fibre 1.9g; Sodium 560mg.

Yam cake

The vegetable on which this Cantonese classic is based inevitably causes confusion. In America it is called taro, where yam can refer to an orange-fleshed sweet potato. What you want for this recipe is the large barrel-shaped vegetable with a hairy brown skin and purple-flecked flesh.

SERVES 6–8

50g/2oz dried shrimp
75ml/5 tbsp vegetable oil
15 shallots, thinly sliced
2 Chinese sausages, diced finely
1kg/2¼lb yam (taro)
300g/11oz/2 cups rice flour
115g/4oz/1 cup tapioca flour
    or 115g/4oz/1 cup cornflour
    (cornstarch)

750ml/1¼ pints/2 cups water
5ml/1 tsp salt
2 spring onions (scallions), plus extra,
    chopped, to garnish
30ml/2 tbsp light soy sauce
30ml/2 tbsp sesame oil
2.5ml/½ tsp ground black pepper
chilli dipping sauce,
    for serving

1 Put the dried shrimp in a bowl and pour over water to cover. Soak for 1 hour, until soft. Heat the oil in a frying pan and fry the shallots for 4–5 minutes, until brown and crisp. Lift out with a slotted spoon and set aside.

2 Drain the soaked shrimp and chop them roughly. Reheat the oil remaining in the pan and fry the shrimp with the diced sausages for 3 minutes. Transfer the shrimp and sausages to a bowl and set aside.

3 Peel the yam and remove the stalk. Cut the flesh into large chunks and place in a steamer placed over simmering water. Steam for 20 minutes until soft.

4 Put the yam into a large bowl and mash with a potato masher. Stir in the rice flour and the tapioca flour or cornflour, then add the water and salt. Mix well.

5 Set aside 30ml/2 tbsp of the fried shallots. Add the remainder to the shrimp mixture. Stir in the spring onions, soy sauce, sesame oil and pepper. Fry gently in a hot wok for 2 minutes.

6 Add the mixture to the mashed yams. Mix well, then press into a lightly oiled steaming tray. Sprinkle the reserved fried shallots over the surface. Steam over rapidly boiling water for 15 minutes. Cool, then cut into wedges, garnish with the reserved fried shallots and spring onions, and serve with the chilli dipping sauce.

Nutritional information per portion: Energy 481kcal/2025kJ; Protein 9.9g; Carbohydrate 79.6g, of which sugars 2.6g; Fat 14.6g, of which saturates 2.9g; Cholesterol 37mg; Calcium 121mg; Fibre 3g; Sodium 648mg.

Pork and peanut wontons with plum sauce

These crispy filled wontons are irresistible served with a sweet plum dipping sauce. The wontons can be filled and set aside for up to eight hours before they are cooked.

MAKES 40–50

175g/6oz/1½ cups minced (ground)
    pork or 175g/6oz pork
    sausages, skinned
2 spring onions (scallions), finely chopped
30ml/2 tbsp peanut butter
10ml/2 tsp oyster sauce (optional)
40–50 wonton skins
30ml/2 tbsp flour paste
vegetable oil, for deep-frying
salt and ground black pepper
lettuce and radishes, to garnish

FOR THE PLUM SAUCE
225g/8oz/generous ¾ cup dark
    plum jam
15ml/1 tbsp rice or white wine vinegar
15ml/1 tbsp dark soy sauce
2.5ml/½ tsp chilli sauce

1 Combine the minced pork or skinned sausages, spring onions, peanut butter, oyster sauce, if using, and seasoning, and then set aside.

2 For the sauce, combine the plum jam, vinegar, soy and chilli sauces in a serving bowl and set aside.

3 To fill the wonton skins, place eight wrappers at a time on a work surface, moisten the edges with the flour paste and place 2.5ml/½ tsp of the filling on each one. Fold in half, corner to corner, and twist.

4 Fill a wok or deep fryer one-third with vegetable oil and heat to 190°C/375°F. Have ready a wire strainer or frying basket and a tray lined with kitchen paper. Drop the wontons, eight at a time, into the hot fat and then fry until they are golden all over, for about 1–2 minutes. Lift out on to the paper-lined tray, using the strainer or basket, and sprinkle with fine salt.

5 Serve the wontons with the plum sauce, garnished with the lettuce and radishes.

Nutritional information per portion: Energy 56kcal/236kJ; Protein 1.5g; Carbohydrate 7.9g, of which sugars 4.1g; Fat 2.3g, of which saturates 0.4g; Cholesterol 3mg; Calcium 8mg; Fibre 0.2g; Sodium 35mg.

Minced pork and taro puffs

A dim sum favourite, these make a morelsh savoury snack. Look for the taro that has light purple flesh with dark specks, as it has the best flavour and Is starchy enough to make a stiff dough.

SERVES 4

cornflour (cornstarch), for dusting
vegetable oil, for deep-frying
salt and ground black pepper

FOR THE PASTRY

500g/1¼lb taro
30ml/2 tbsp plain (all-purpose) flour
15ml/1 tbsp lard
pinch of bicarbonate of soda (baking soda)
15ml/1 tbsp sesame oil
5ml/1 tsp sugar

FOR THE FILLING

150g/5oz minced (ground) pork
5ml/1 tsp cornflour (cornstarch)
30ml/2 tbsp vegetable oil
30ml/2 tbsp frozen peas
5g/1 tsp sugar
15ml/1 tbsp sesame oil

1 To make the pastry, peel the taro and cut it into chunks. Steam for about 15 minutes until soft. Mash while still warm and mix with the remaining pastry ingredients and seasoning to form a dough.

2 Turn out on to a lightly floured board and knead until the dough is soft and pliable. Set it aside while you make the filling, covered with a damp dish towel to prevent it drying out.

3 Mix the pork with the cornflour and moisten with a little water.

4 Heat the vegetable oil in a pan and fry the pork gently until nearly cooked. Stir in all of the other filling ingredients and seasoning.

5 Remove from the heat and leave to cool a little. Meanwhile, divide the dough into four portions and roll out into flat rounds.

6 Fill each round with 15ml/1 tbsp of the pork mixture. Shape into an oval pasty, sealing the pastry well around the filling. Dust each parcel with cornflour and deep-fry until golden brown. Serve immediately.

Nutritional information per portion: Energy 367kcal/1541kJ; Protein 11.2g; Carbohydrate 45.7g, of which sugars 3.8g; Fat 16.8g, of which saturates 3.7g; Cholesterol 27mg; Calcium 36mg; Fibre 2.2g; Sodium 30mg.

Steamed pork buns

These deliciously light stuffed buns are a popular street snack sold throughout China. The soft texture of the bun contrasts wonderfully with the spiced meat filling inside. They make an unusual alternative to rice and, once cooked, can be reheated in the steamer.

SERVES 4

30ml/2 tbsp golden caster
    (superfine) sugar
10ml/2 tsp dried yeast
300g/11oz/2³/₄ cups plain
    (all-purpose) flour
30ml/2 tbsp sunflower oil
10ml/2 tsp baking powder

FOR THE FILLING

250g/9oz pork sausages
15ml/1 tbsp barbecue sauce
30ml/2 tbsp oyster sauce
15ml/1 tbsp sweet chilli sauce
15ml/1 tbsp rice wine
15ml/1 tbsp hoisin sauce
5ml/1 tsp chilli oil

1 To make the dough, pour 250ml/8fl oz/1 cup warm water into a mixing bowl. Add the sugar and stir to dissolve. Stir in the yeast, cover and leave in a warm place for 15 minutes.

2 Sift the flour into a large mixing bowl and make a well in the centre. Add the sugar and yeast mixture to it with the sunflower oil. Fold the mixture together using your fingers and turn out on to a lightly floured surface.

3 Knead the dough for 8–10 minutes until smooth and elastic. Place in a lightly oiled bowl, cover with a dish towel and leave to rise in a warm place for 3–4 hours.

4 When risen, place the dough on a lightly floured surface, punch down and shape into a large circle. Sprinkle the baking powder in the centre, bring all the edges towards the centre and knead for 6–8 minutes. Divide the dough into 12 balls, cover with a clean, damp dish towel and set aside.

5 Squeeze the sausage meat from the casings into a large bowl and stir in the barbecue sauce, oyster sauce, sweet chilli sauce, rice wine, hoisin sauce and chilli oil. Mix thoroughly, using your fingers to combine.

6 Press each dough ball to form a round, 12cm/4¹/₂in in diameter. Place a large spoonful of the pork mixture in the centre of each round and bring the edges up to the centre, press together to seal and form a bun shape.

7 Arrange the buns on several layers of a large bamboo steamer, cover and steam over a wok of simmering water for 20–25 minutes, or until they are puffed up and the pork is cooked through. Serve immediately.

Nutritional information per portion: Energy 159kcal/664kJ; Protein 13.5g; Carbohydrate 10.6g, of which sugars 0.4g; Fat 6.9g, of which saturates 1.7g; Cholesterol 157mg; Calcium 46mg; Fibre 0g; Sodium 526mg.

Pork and prawn dumplings

While dim sum are generally attributed to southern China, these morsels are enjoyed throughout the entire country. Pork is the main ingredient here, but there are also seafood versions.

SERVES 4

100g/3³/₄oz raw prawns (shrimp), peeled
   and deveined
2 spring onions (scallions)
225g/8oz/1 cup minced (ground) pork
30ml/2 tbsp light soy sauce
15ml/1 tbsp sesame oil
2.5ml/¹/₂ tsp ground black pepper
15ml/1 tbsp cornflour (cornstarch)
16 round wonton wrappers
16 large garden peas, thawed if frozen
chilli sauce, for dipping

COOK'S TIP

If you can only find square wonton wrappers, trim off the corners to make a rough circle before filling them.

1 Chop the prawns finely to make a coarse paste. This can be done using a sharp knife or in a food processor, but if you use a food processor use the pulse button, or the prawns will become rubbery. Scrape into a bowl.

2 Chop the spring onions very finely. Add them to the puréed prawns, with the pork, soy sauce, sesame oil, pepper and cornflour. Mix well.

3 Holding a wonton wrapper on the palm of one hand, spoon a heaped teaspoon of the filling into the centre. Cup your hand so that the wrapper enfolds the filling to make the classic dumpling shape. Leave the top slightly open. Top the gap with a pea. Fill the remaining wonton wrappers in the same way.

4 Place the dumplings on a lightly oiled plate and steam over a wok of rapidly boiling water for 10 minutes. Serve with a chilli sauce dip.

Nutritional information per portion: Energy 228kcal/957kJ; Protein 18.2g; Carbohydrate 20.2g, of which sugars 1.3g; Fat 8.8g, of which saturates 2.5g; Cholesterol 86mg; Calcium 57mg; Fibre 1.3g; Sodium 622mg.

Butterfly prawns

A classic Cantonese restaurant dish, these prawns are dipped in a very light batter, almost like tempura, and then quickly cooked in very hot oil until golden and crispy.

SERVES 4

16 large prawns (shrimp)
30ml/2 tbsp plain (all-purpose) flour
15ml/1 tbsp self-raising
    (self-rising) flour
a pinch of bicarbonate of soda
    (baking soda)
15ml/1 tbsp sesame oil
120ml/4fl oz/¹/₂ cup cold water
vegetable oil, for deep-frying
chilli and garlic dipping sauce,
    to serve

1 Clean the prawns and shell them, but leave the tails intact. Using a sharp knife, slit each prawn halfway through the back, then spread them flat so that they resemble butterflies.

2 Mix the plain flour and self-raising flour in a bowl. Add the bicarbonate of soda, then the sesame oil and cold water. Stir to make a smooth batter.

3 Heat the oil in a wok or deep-fryer to 190°C/375°F. Dip each prawn in turn in the batter, gently shaking off the excess, and add to the hot oil. Repeat with more prawns, but do not overcrowd the wok or fryer.

4 After 2–3 minutes, when the prawns are golden brown, lift them out and drain on kitchen paper. Serve hot, with the chilli and garlic dipping sauce.

Nutritional information per portion: Energy 156kcal/653kJ; Protein 12.5g; Carbohydrate 7.3g, of which sugars 0.5g; Fat 8.0g, of which saturates 1.3g, Cholesterol 157mg; Calcium 64mg; Fibre 0.3g; Sodium 310mg.

Prawn and sesame toasts

These little triangles are a popular hot snack, making use of the white bread introduced to China by European settlers. They are surprisingly easy to prepare and you can cook them in a few minutes.

SERVES 4

225g/8oz peeled raw prawns (shrimp)
15ml/1 tbsp sherry
15ml/1 tbsp soy sauce
2 egg whites, whisked until stiff
30ml/2 tbsp cornflour (cornstarch)
4 slices white bread
115g/4oz/¹/₂ cup sesame seeds
vegetable oil, for deep-frying
sweet chilli sauce, to serve

1 Process the prawns, sherry and soy sauce in a food processor. Add the egg whites and cornflour and lightly fold them together until well blended.

2 Cut each slice of bread into four triangles. Lay the sesame seeds on a large plate.

3 Spread the prawn paste over one side of each bread triangle, then press into the sesame seeds.

4 Heat the oil in a wok or deep-fryer, to 190°C/375°F or until a cube of bread, added to the oil, browns in about 40 seconds. Add the toasts, a few at a time, prawn side down, and deep-fry for 2–3 minutes, then turn and fry on the other side until golden.

5 Drain on kitchen paper and serve immediately with the sweet chilli sauce for dipping.

Nutritional information per portion: Energy 433kcal/1806kJ; Protein 19.1g; Carbohydrate 27.7g, of which sugars 1.2g; Fat 27.6g, of which saturates 3.6g; Cholesterol 110mg; Calcium 271mg; Fibre 2.7g; Sodium 559mg.

Steamed crab dim sum with Chinese chives

These delectable Chinese dumplings have a wonderfully sticky texture and make a perfect appetizer. You can make them in advance, storing them in the refrigerator until ready to cook.

SERVES 4

150g/5oz fresh white crab meat
115g/4oz minced (ground) pork
30ml/2 tbsp chopped Chinese chives
15ml/1 tbsp finely chopped red
**   (bell) pepper**
30ml/2 tbsp sweet chilli sauce
30ml/2 tbsp hoisin sauce
24 fresh dumpling wrappers (available
**   from Asian stores)**
Chinese chives, to garnish
chilli oil and soy sauce, to serve

1 Place the crab meat, pork and chopped chives in a bowl. Add the red pepper, sweet chilli and hoisin sauces and mix well to combine.

2 Put a small spoonful of the mixture into the centre of each wrapper. Brush the edges of each wrapper with water and fold over to form a half-moon shape. Press and pleat the edges to seal. Tap the base of each dumpling to flatten it.

3 Arrange the dumplings on lightly oiled plates and fit inside the tiers of a bamboo steamer. Cover the steamer and place over a wok of simmering water. Steam for 8–10 minutes, or until the dumplings are cooked through and slightly translucent.

4 Divide the dumplings among four plates. Garnish with Chinese chives and serve immediately with chilli oil and soy sauce for dipping.

Nutritional information per portion: Energy 166kcal/700kJ; Protein 14.7g; Carbohydrate 20.5g, of which sugars 1.4g. Fat 3.3g, of which saturates 1.1g; Cholesterol 46mg; Calcium 83mg; Fibre 0.8g; Sodium 287mg.

Crab tofu parcels

This is an innovative way to use crab meat and is a staple dish in many Chinese restaurants. Most long-life tofu comes in two types, soft and firm. Use the firm variety for these parcels.

SERVES 4

150g/5oz fresh or canned crab meat
5ml/1 tsp cornflour (cornstarch)
1 egg, lightly beaten
15ml/1 tbsp sesame oil
2 packets firm tofu, about 500g/1¼lb
2 spring onions (scallions), trimmed and
    finely chopped
salt and ground black pepper

1 Lightly crush the crab meat and mix to a paste with the cornflour and beaten egg.

2 Add salt, pepper and the sesame oil and mix thoroughly.

3 Divide the tofu into 4 square pieces. With a melon baller, gently scoop out a hollow in each piece.

4 Fill each hollow with the crab meat mixture and place in a deep plate. Sprinkle each piece with finely chopped spring onion.

5 Place the parcels on to lightly-oiled plates and transfer to a bamboo steamer. Steam the parcels for 5 minutes over a wok of boiling water and serve as a warm appetizer.

Nutritional information per portion: Energy 170kcal/706kJ; Protein 18.6g; Carbohydrate 2g, of which sugars 0.5g; Fat 9.8g, of which saturates 1.5g; Cholesterol 75mg; Calcium 692mg; Fibre 0.1g; Sodium 230mg.

Wenchang steamed crab

A small town on the east coast of Hainan Island in Southern China, Wenchang is famed for its excellent seafood. Preparing crab can be a little fiddly, but the end result is worth the effort.

SERVES 4

4 whole crabs, about 250g/9oz each
15ml/1 tbsp chopped fresh root ginger
30ml/2 tbsp rice wine
15ml/1 tbsp light soy sauce
5ml/1 tsp ground black pepper
chilli and garlic sauce, for dipping

VARIATION
The liquor that collects at the bottom of the plate or bowl in any steamed shellfish dish is delicious when mixed with rice.

1 Clean the crabs and remove the belly flap from each. Prise the shell away from the body and cut each crab into four pieces. Crack the large claws for easy removal of the meat after the crabs are cooked.

2 Mix the ginger, rice wine, soy sauce and pepper in a heatproof bowl which will both accomodate all of the crabs and go in a steamer.

3 Place the bowl into a steamer and cook the prepared crabs over boiling water for about 15 minutes or until they turn pink all over.

4 Serve the hot crabs immediately, with a chilli and garlic sauce on the side for dipping. Or allow to cool and serve the delicately spiced flesh as part of an impressive Chinese dinner-party salad.

Nutritional information per portion: 119kcal/495kJ; Protein 17.1g; Carbohydrate 0.4g, of which sugars 0.3g; Fat 4.8g, of which saturates 0.5g; Cholesterol 63mg; Calcium 1mg; Fibre 0g; Sodium 642mg.

Clams with chilli and yellow bean sauce

This delicious dish is simple to prepare yet deceptively impressive, making it an ideal dinner-party dish. It can be made in a matter of minutes so will not keep you away from your guests for very long.

SERVES 4–6

1kg/2¼lb fresh clams
30ml/2 tbsp vegetable oil
4 garlic cloves, finely chopped
15ml/1 tbsp grated fresh root ginger
4 shallots, finely chopped
30ml/2 tbsp yellow bean sauce
6 red chillies, seeded and chopped
15ml/1 tbsp fish sauce
a pinch of sugar
a handful of basil leaves, plus extra
   to garnish

1 Wash and scrub the clams. Heat the oil in a wok or large frying pan. Add the garlic and ginger and fry for about 30 seconds, add the shallots and fry for a further minute.

2 Add the scrubbed clams to the pan. Using a fish slice or metal spatula, turn them a few times to coat all over with the oil. Add the yellow bean sauce and half the chopped red chillies.

3 Continue to cook, stirring often, for 5–7 minutes, or until all the clams are open. (Discard any that fail to open.) Adjust the seasoning with the fish sauce and a little sugar. Finally add the basil leaves and stir to mix.

4 Transfer the clams to a serving platter. Garnish with the remaining chopped red chillies and basil leaves and serve.

Nutritional information per portion: Energy 94kcal/393kJ; Protein 11.6g; Carbohydrate 2.4g, of which sugars 0.6g; Fat 4.3g, of which saturates 0.6g; Cholesterol 45mg; Calcium 75mg; Fibre 0.7g; Sodium 998mg.

Crispy salt and pepper squid

These tempting morsels of squid look stunning skewered on small or large wooden sticks and are perfect served with drinks, or as an appetizer. Serve piping hot straight from the wok.

SERVES 4

750g/1lb 10oz fresh squid, cleaned
juice of 4–5 lemons
15ml/1 tbsp ground black pepper
15ml/1 tbsp salt
10ml/2 tsp caster (superfine) sugar
115g/4oz/1 cup cornflour (cornstarch)
3 egg whites, lightly beaten
vegetable oil, for deep-frying
chilli sauce or sweet-and-sour sauce,
    for dipping
skewers or cocktail sticks (toothpicks),
    to serve

1 Cut the squid into large bitesize pieces and score a diamond pattern on each piece.

2 Trim the tentacles. Place in a large mixing bowl and pour over the lemon juice. Cover and marinate for 10–15 minutes. Drain well and pat dry.

3 In a mixing bowl mix together the pepper, salt, sugar and cornflour.

4 Dip the squid pieces in the egg whites and then toss lightly in the seasoned flour, shaking off any excess.

5 Fill a wok one-third full of oil and heat to 180°C/350°F. (A cube of bread, dropped into the oil, should brown in 45 seconds.) Working in batches, deep-fry the squid for 1 minute. Drain and serve threaded on to skewers, with chilli sauce.

Nutritional information per portion: Energy 346kcal/1462kJ; Protein 31.2g; Carbohydrate 31.3g, of which sugars 2.0g; Fat 11.6g, of which saturates 1.0g, Cholesterol 422mg, Calcium 35mg, Fibre 0g, Sodium 174 mg.

Rice & noodles

Staples throughout Asia, rice and

noodles form the basis of many Chinese

meals. This chapter features classic

recipes that make the best use of

these simple ingredients, with magical

results. Try the ever-popular Special

Fried Rice or Vegetable Noodles with

Yellow Bean Sauce, or for a

sophisticated dinner party, Lobster

Noodles or Lotus Leaf Rice.

Rice with mixed vegetables

This Chinese staple originally called for ten different greens to be cooked with the rice. The tradition doesn't have to be followed exactly, but try to use several vegetables, plus meat for extra flavour.

SERVES 4

4 dried shiitake mushrooms
150ml/¼ pint/⅔ cup boiling water
30ml/2 tbsp vegetable oil
2 garlic cloves, chopped
150g/5oz lean pork, finely sliced
150g/5oz pak choi (bok choy),
    finely sliced
30ml/2 tbsp peas, thawed
    if frozen
30ml/2 tbsp light soy sauce
5ml/1 tsp ground black pepper
5ml/1 tsp cornflour (cornstarch) mixed
    to a paste with 15ml/1 tbsp
    cold water
800g/1¾lb/7 cups cooked rice

1 Put the mushrooms in a heatproof bowl and pour over the boiling water. Leave to soak for 20–30 minutes, until soft. Using a slotted spoon, transfer the mushrooms to a board. Cut off and discard the stems. Chop the caps finely. Strain the soaking liquid into a bowl and set aside.

2 Heat the oil in a wok, add the garlic and fry over medium heat for 40 seconds, until light brown.

3 Add the pork to the wok and fry for a further 2 minutes. Add the pak choi, peas and mushrooms. Stir to mix, then add the soy sauce, black pepper and the mushroom soaking liquid. Cook, stirring frequently, for 4 minutes.

4 Add the cornflour paste and stir until the mixture thickens slightly. Finally stir in the cooked rice. As soon as it is piping hot, spoon the mixture into a heated bowl and serve.

Nutritional information per portion: Energy 199kcal/834kJ; Protein 4.6g; Carbohydrate 43.4g, of which sugars 6.6g; Fat 0.7g, of which saturates 0.1g; Cholesterol 0mg; Calcium 23mg; Fibre 1.6g; Sodium 232mg.

Vegetable noodles with yellow bean sauce

Yellow bean sauce is made from fermented yellow beans and has a marvellous texture and spicy, aromatic flavour. Be careful not to add too much, because it is very salty.

SERVES 4

50g/5oz thin egg noodles
200g/7oz/1½ cups baby courgettes (zucchini), halved lengthways
200g/7oz sugarsnap peas, trimmed
200g/7oz/1¾ cups shelled peas
200g/7oz/1¾ cups baby leeks, sliced lengthways
15ml/1 tbsp sunflower oil
5 garlic cloves, sliced
45ml/3 tbsp yellow bean sauce
45ml/3 tbsp sweet chilli sauce
30ml/2 tbsp sweet soy sauce
cashew nuts, to garnish

1 Cook the noodles as per the packet instructions, drain and set aside.

2 Line a bamboo steamer with baking parchment and place the leeks, peas and courgettes in it. Cover and steam over a wok of boiling water for 5 minutes, then remove and set aside.

3 Empty and dry the wok. Add the oil to the wok and place over a medium heat. Add the garlic and stir-fry for 1–2 minutes.

4 Mix together the yellow bean, sweet chilli and soy sauces, then pour into the wok. Stir to mix with the garlic, then add the vegetables and noodles and toss together. Cook for 2–3 minutes, stirring frequently, until heated through.

5 To serve, divide the vegetable noodles among four warmed serving bowls and and sprinkle over the cashew nuts to garnish.

Nutritional information per portion: Energy 296kcal/1241kJ; Protein 14.2g; Carbohydrate 44.9g, of which sugars 7.4g; Fat 7.8g, of which saturates 1.6g; Cholesterol 11mg; Calcium 61mg; Fibre 8.2g; Sodium 209mg.

Special fried rice

More colourful and elaborate than other fried rice dishes, special fried rice is a meal in itself.
Cook the rice well in advance and allow to cool before cooking this dish.

SERVES 4

50g/2oz/¹⁄₃ cup cooked peeled prawns (shrimp)

3 eggs

5ml/1 tsp salt

2 spring onions (scallions), finely chopped

60ml/4 tbsp vegetable oil

115g/4oz lean pork, finely diced

15ml/1 tbsp light soy sauce

15ml/1 tbsp rice wine

450g/1lb/6 cups cooked rice

115g/4oz shelled peas

1 Pat the prawns dry with kitchen paper. Put the eggs in a bowl with a pinch of the salt and a few pieces of spring onion. Whisk lightly.

2 Heat half the oil in a wok, add the pork and stir-fry until golden. Add the prawns and cook for 1 minute, then add the soy sauce and rice wine. Spoon the pork and prawn mixture into a bowl and keep hot.

3 Heat the remaining vegetable oil in the wok and, when hot, pour in the eggs and lightly scramble them. Add the cooked rice and stir well to distribute the egg throughout.

4 Add the remaining salt, spring onions, peas, and the stir-fried prawns and pork. Toss well over the heat to thoroughly combine and serve either hot or cold.

Nutritional information per portion: Energy 343kcal/1434kJ; Protein 20.2g; Carbohydrate 40.5g, of which sugars 4.2g; Fat 11.2g, of which saturates 1.6g; Cholesterol 124mg; Calcium 91mg; Fibre 2.4g; Sodium 632mg.

Fragrant Harbour fried rice

This tasty and substantial rice dish is packed with ingredients, but is quick to make. Its name is derived from the Chinese name for Hong Kong, which translates as Fragrant Harbour.

SERVES 4

about 90ml/6 tbsp vegetable oil
2 eggs, beaten
8 shallots, sliced
115g/4oz/²/₃ cup cooked peeled prawns
   (shrimp)
3 garlic cloves, crushed
115g/4oz cooked pork, cut into
   thin strips
4 dried Chinese mushrooms, soaked,
   stems removed and sliced
115g/4oz Chinese sausage, cooked and
   sliced at an angle
225g/8oz/generous 1 cup long grain rice,
   cooked, cooled quickly and chilled
30ml/2 tbsp light soy sauce
115g/4oz/1 cup frozen peas, thawed
2 spring onions (scallions), shredded
salt and ground black pepper
coriander (cilantro) leaves,
   to garnish

1 Heat 15ml/1 tbsp of the oil in a frying pan, add the eggs and cook until just set. Slide the omelette out, roll it up and cut into strips. Set aside.

2 Heat a wok, add 15ml/1 tbsp of the oil and fry the shallots until golden. Remove and set aside. Fry the prawns and garlic for 1 minute, then remove.

3 Add 15ml/1 tbsp more oil to the wok and stir-fry the pork and mushrooms for 2 minutes.

4 Add the Chinese sausage slices and heat for 2 minutes. Lift the ingredients out of the wok and keep warm.

5 Stir-fry the rice in the remaining oil until it glistens. Stir in the soy sauce, salt and pepper, plus half the cooked ingredients. Add the peas and half the spring onions and toss until the peas are cooked. Pile the fried rice on a platter, top with the remaining ingredients and garnish with coriander leaves and spring onions.

Nutritional information per portion: Energy 450kcal/1072kJ; Protein 14.5g; Carbohydrate 51g, of which sugars 4.4g; Fat 20.9g, of which saturates 3.1g; Cholesterol 113mg; Calcium 40mg; Fibre 1.1g; Sodium 58mg.

Noodles with sesame-roasted spring onions

You can use any kind of noodles for this dish, rice noodles look and taste particularly good, but egg noodles work very well too. It's delicious served with fish and chicken dishes.

SERVES 4

1 bunch of spring onions (scallions), trimmed
30ml/2 tbsp sesame oil
225g/8oz flat rice or egg noodles
30ml/2 tbsp oyster sauce
salt and ground black pepper

1 Preheat the oven to 200°C/ 400°F/Gas 6. Cut the spring onions into three pieces, then put them in a small roasting pan and season with salt and pepper.

2 Drizzle the sesame oil over the spring onions and roast for 10 minutes, until they are slightly charred and tender. Set aside.

3 Cook the rice or egg noodles according to the instructions on the packet and drain thoroughly.

4 Toss the noodles with the spring onions and oyster sauce, making sure to coat the noodles in the sauce as this will prevent them from sticking. Season with ground black pepper. Serve immediately.

Nutritional information per portion: Energy 44kcal/184kJ; Protein 3.3g; Carbohydrate 0.2g, of which sugars 0.1g; Fat 2.9g, of which saturates 0.8g; Cholesterol 95mg; Calcium 18mg; Fibre 0.1g; Sodium 166mg.

Jewelled vegetable rice with crispy fried eggs

This vibrant, colourful stir-fry is a real feast for the senses and makes a tasty light meal.
Alternatively, serve it as an accompaniment to simply grilled meat or fish.

SERVES 4

30ml/2 tbsp sunflower oil
2 garlic cloves, finely chopped
4 red Asian shallots, thinly sliced
1 small red chilli, finely sliced
90g/3¹/₂oz/ generous ¹/₂ cup carrots,
   cut into matchsticks
90g/3¹/₂oz/generous ¹/₂ cup fine green
   beans, cut into 2cm/³/₄in lengths
90g/3¹/₂oz/1 cup fresh corn
1 red (bell) pepper, seeded and cut into
   1cm/¹/₂in dice
90g/3¹/₂oz button (white) mushrooms
500g/1¹/₄lb cooked, cooled long grain rice
45ml/3 tbsp light soy sauce
10ml/2 tsp green curry paste
4 crispy fried eggs, salad leaves and
   lime wedges, to serve

1 Heat the sunflower oil in a wok over a high heat. When hot, add the garlic, shallots and chilli. Stir-fry for about 2 minutes.

2 Add the carrots, green beans, corn, red pepper and mushrooms to the wok and stir-fry for 3–4 minutes. Add the cooked, cooled rice and stir-fry for a further 4–5 minutes.

3 Mix together the light soy sauce and curry paste and add to the wok. Toss to mix in well with the rice and vegetables and stir-fry for 2–3 minutes until piping hot. Ladle the rice into four bowls or plates and top each portion with a crispy fried egg. Serve with crisp green salad leaves and wedges of lime to squeeze over.

Nutritional information per portion: Energy 392kcal/1648kJ; Protein 13.6g; Carbohydrate 51.4g, of which sugars 8.2g; Fat 16.1g, of which saturates 3.6g; Cholesterol 261mg; Calcium 79mg; Fibre 2.1g; Sodium 968mg.

Mushroom clay pot rice

Clay pots are very handy as they can go straight from the fire to the table. If you are worried that your pot may crack, cook the rice in a wok or pan and transfer it to an oven-warmed clay pot to serve.

SERVES 4

250g/9oz/1¼ cups jasmine rice

400ml/14fl oz/1⅔ cups water

30ml/2 tbsp vegetable oil

15ml/1 tbsp sesame oil

8 dried shiitake mushrooms, soaked until
    soft, or 8 canned shiitake mushrooms

3 garlic cloves, crushed

30g/2 tbsp oyster sauce

5ml/1 tsp ground black pepper

COOK'S TIP

To season a clay pot and prevent cracking, fill with water and bring to the boil. Simmer for 10 minutes, then leave to cool. Pour out the water and wipe the pot dry.

1 Place the rice in a pan with the water, bring to the boil and simmer, tightly covered, for about 20 minutes, until the water is absorbed. Remove from the heat and leave to steam for 10 minutes.

2 While the rice is cooking, slice the mushrooms into strips. Heat the oil in a wok and fry the garlic until golden. Add the mushrooms and stir-fry for 2 minutes.

3 Add the oyster sauce and the black pepper. Pour in 100ml/3½fl oz/scant ½ cup water and stir for 2 minutes. Heat a clay pot in a hot oven for 10 minutes.

4 About 5 minutes before the rice is done, pile the mushrooms on top and cover the pan to finish cooking.

5 Remove the warmed clay pot from the oven and transfer the rice and mushroom mixture to it to serve.

Nutritional information per portion: Energy 315kcal/1312kJ; Protein 5.3g; Carbohydrate 53.2g, of which sugars 3.2g; Fat 8.7g, of which saturates 1.1g; Cholesterol 0mg; Calcium 15mg; Fibre 0.4g; Sodium 185mg.

Chinese clay pot rice with chicken

This Cantonese dish is a great family one-pot meal. The traditional clay pot ensures that the ingredients remain moist, while allowing the flavours to mingle.

SERVES 4

500g/1¼ lb chicken breast fillets
5 dried shiitake mushrooms, soaked in
    hot water for 30 minutes
1 Chinese sausage, sliced
750ml/1¼pints/3 cups chicken stock
225g/8oz/generous 1 cup long grain rice
fresh coriander (cilantro) leaves, finely
    chopped, to garnish

FOR THE MARINADE

30ml/2 tbsp sesame oil
45ml/3 tbsp oyster sauce
30ml/2 tbsp soy sauce
25g/1oz fresh root ginger, finely grated
2 spring onions (scallions), finely sliced
1 red chilli, seeded and finely sliced
5ml/1 tsp sugar

1 In a bowl, mix together the ingredients for the marinade. Cut the chicken into thin strips and toss it in the marinade. Set aside.

2 Squeeze the shiitake mushrooms to get rid of any excess water. Using a sharp knife, remove any hard stems from the mushrooms and cut the caps in half. Add the caps and the Chinese sausage to the chicken.

3 Bring the stock to a boil in the clay pot. Stir in the rice and bring it back to the boil. Reduce the heat, cover the pot, and leave to simmer on a low heat for 15–20 minutes, until almost all the liquid has been absorbed.

4 Spread the marinated mixture over the top of the rice and cover the pot. Leave to steam for about 15 minutes, until all the liquid is absorbed and the chicken is cooked. Garnish the rice with chopped coriander and serve at once.

Nutritional information per portion: Energy 371kcal/1560kJ; Protein 36.2g; Carbohydrate 46.8g, of which sugars 1g; Fat 4g, of which saturates 1.2g; Cholesterol 93mg; Calcium 54mg; Fibre 0.7g; Sodium 721mg.

Hainanese chicken rice

This Hainanese recipe focuses on an unusual steeping process to ensure smooth, silky chicken, which is accompanied by aromatic rice, a bowl of chicken broth, soy sauce for dipping and a garnish of crunchy spring onions and cucumber, and a delicious ginger and chilli sambal.

SERVES 4–6

1 chicken (1.25kg/2¹/₂lb), cleaned
30ml/2 tbsp light soy sauce
15ml/1 tbsp rice wine
50g/2oz fresh root ginger, peeled, thickly sliced
  and crushed
4 garlic cloves, lightly crushed
2 spring onions (scallions), crushed
1.5 litres/2¹/₂ pints/
  6¹/₄ cups chicken stock
10ml/2 tsp sesame oil
225g/8oz/generous 1 cup jasmine rice,
  rinsed and drained
salt and ground black pepper

FOR THE SAMBAL
10 red chillies, seeded and chopped
6 garlic cloves, chopped
25g/1oz fresh root ginger, peeled and chopped
15ml/1 tbsp sesame or groundnut (peanut) oil
15–30ml/1–2 tbsp fresh lime juice
10ml/2 tsp sugar

TO SERVE
fresh coriander (cilantro) leaves
dark soy sauce
1 small cucumber, halved lengthways and finely sliced
3 spring onions, trimmed and sliced

1 Rub the chicken, inside and out, with 15ml/1 tbsp soy sauce and the rice wine. Place the ginger, garlic and spring onions in the cavity. Leave for 30 minutes.

2 Immerse the chicken in boiling stock in a deep pan. Bring back to the boil, cover the pan and remove from the heat.

3 Leave the chicken to steep for 15 minutes. Lift the chicken to drain the cavity, reheat the stock to boiling point, cover the pan and steep the chicken in the stock, off the heat, for a further 15 minutes. Repeat the process every 15 minutes, until the chicken has steeped for a total of 1 hour.

4 Lift the chicken out of the stock, and plunge it into a bowl of iced water. Bring the stock back to the boil. Drain the chicken, trim off the wings, neck and legs, and add them to the stock. Rub the remaining 15ml/1 tbsp soy sauce and the sesame oil over the chicken and set aside.

5 Keep the stock simmering, skim off any fat from the top and season. Measure 550ml/18fl oz/2¹/₂ cups of the stock and pour into a separate pan. Cover the remaining stock and keep it barely simmering. Bring the measured stock to the boil and add the rice. Stir once, reduce the heat and simmer until the stock is absorbed. Remove from the heat, cover with a dish towel, then the lid, and stand for 15 minutes.

6 To prepare the sambal, grind the chillies, garlic and ginger to a smooth paste in a food processor. Bind with the oil and lime juice, and stir in the sugar. Spoon into individual dipping bowls.

7 To serve, remove the chicken skin and separate the meat from the bones. Slice the thighs and breasts into bitesize pieces. Place the chicken on a platter and garnish with a few coriander leaves. Give each person a mound of rice. Place the bowls of sambal on each plate, along with individual bowls of dark soy sauce, slices of cucumber and a few coriander leaves. Ladle the hot chicken broth into warmed serving bowls and sprinkle spring onions over the top. Place a plate of rice and sauces, and bowl of broth, in front of each person, and set the chicken in the middle of the table.

Nutritional information per portion: Energy 460kcal/1913kJ; Protein 28.6g; Carbohydrate 30.4g, of which sugars 0.4g; Fat 24.6g, of which saturates 6.7g; Cholesterol 133mg; Calcium 37mg; Fibre 0.5g; Sodium 108mg.

Chicken chow mein

Chow mein is arguably the best-known Chinese noodle dish in the West and is a staple of Chinese restaurants. Noodles are stir-fried with meat, seafood or vegetables.

SERVES 4

350g/12oz medium egg noodles
225g/8oz skinless, boneless
    chicken breasts
45ml/3 tbsp soy sauce
15ml/1 tbsp rice wine or dry sherry
15ml/1 tbsp dark sesame oil
60ml/4 tbsp vegetable oil
2 garlic cloves, finely chopped
50g/2oz/¹/₃ cup mangetouts, topped
    and tailed
115g/4oz/¹/₂ cup beansprouts
50g/2oz ham, finely shredded
4 spring onions (scallions), finely chopped
salt and ground black pepper

1 Cook the noodles in a pan of boiling water until tender. Drain, rinse under cold water and drain well.

2 Slice the chicken into fine shreds about 5cm/2in in length. Place in a bowl and add 10ml/2 tsp of the soy sauce, the rice wine or sherry and sesame oil.

3 Heat half the vegetable oil in a wok or large frying pan over a high heat. Add the chicken mixture and stir-fry for 2 minutes, set aside and keep warm.

4 Wipe the wok clean and heat the remaining oil. Stir in the garlic, mangetouts, beansprouts and ham, stir-fry for another minute and add the noodles.

5 Continue to stir-fry until the noodles are heated through. Add the remaining soy sauce and season with salt and pepper. Return the chicken and any juices to the noodle mixture. Stir in the spring onions, and serve at once.

Nutritional information per portion: Energy 593kcal/2494kJ; Protein 31.1g; Carbohydrate 69.7g, of which sugars 4.4g; Fat 22.6g, of which saturates 2.7g; Cholesterol 44mg; Calcium 44mg; Fibre 3.4g; Sodium 995mg.

Lotus leaf rice

This dish is eaten on festive occasions but is also a popular dim sum item in restaurants. Lotus seeds are added for flavour and texture as well as for symbolic reasons, as they represent fertility.

SERVES 4

250g/9oz/1¼ cups sticky (glutinous) rice, soaked for at least 2 hours, then drained
250ml/8fl oz/1 cup water
10ml/2 tsp salt
2 large lotus leaves

FOR THE FILLING

150g/5oz chicken breast, diced
4 dried Chinese (shiitake) mushrooms, soaked until soft, or canned mushrooms
30ml/2 tbsp vegetable oil
3 garlic cloves, crushed
30ml/2 tbsp oyster sauce
5ml/1 tsp ground black pepper
15ml/1 tbsp sesame oil
45ml/3 tbsp water
20 canned lotus seeds

1 Put the soaked rice in a steamer, add the water and salt and steam for 20 minutes. Set aside to cool.

2 Cut each mushroom into quarters. Heat the oil in a wok or frying pan and stir-fry the garlic until golden. Add the chicken and stir-fry for 2 minutes.

3 Add the mushrooms, oyster sauce, lotus seeds, pepper, sesame oil and water and continue to stir-fry until the chicken is completely cooked.

4 Spread out the lotus leaves, laying one on top of the other to prevent leaking. Spread the steamed rice on top, flattening it with a spatula. Spread the chicken and mushrooms evenly over it.

5 Make a firm parcel with the lotus leaves, tucking the ends under to secure. Steam for 5 minutes before serving.

Nutritional information per portion: Energy 377kcal/1581kJ; Protein 20.7g; Carbohydrate 63.7g, of which sugars 2.4g; Fat 4g, of which saturates 1.2g; Cholesterol 43mg; Calcium 31mg; Fibre 0.8g; Sodium 1082mg.

Crispy five-spice chicken
with crunchy vegetable noodles

Tender strips of chicken fillet, with a delicately spiced rice flour coating, become deliciously crisp and golden when fried. They make a great meal served on a bed of stir-fried vegetable noodles.

SERVES 4

200g/7oz thin egg noodles
30ml/2 tbsp sunflower oil
2 garlic cloves, very thinly sliced
1 red chilli, seeded and sliced
1/2 red (bell) pepper, very thinly sliced
300g/11oz carrots, peeled and
    cut into thin strips
300g/11oz kai lan (Chinese broccoli)
    or Chinese leaves (Chinese cabbage),
    roughly sliced

45ml/3 tbsp hoisin sauce
45ml/3 tbsp soy sauce
15ml/1 tbsp sugar
4 chicken breast fillets,
    skinned and cut into strips
2 egg whites, lightly beaten
115g/4oz/1 cup rice flour
15ml/1 tbsp five-spice powder
salt and ground black pepper
vegetable oil, for frying

1 Cook the noodles according to the packet instructions, drain and set aside.

2 Heat the sunflower oil in a wok, then add the garlic, chilli, red pepper, carrots and kai lan or Chinese leaves and stir-fry over a high heat for 2–3 minutes.

3 Add the sauces and sugar to the wok and cook for a further 2–3 minutes. Add the drained noodles, toss to combine, then remove from the heat, cover and keep warm.

4 Dip the chicken strips into the egg white. Combine the rice flour and five-spice powder in a shallow dish and season. Add the chicken strips to the flour mixture and toss to coat.

5 Heat about 2.5cm/1½in oil in a clean wok. When hot, shallow fry the chicken for 3–4 minutes until crisp and golden.

6 To serve, divide the noodle mixture between warmed plates or bowls and top each serving with the chicken.

Nutritional information per portion: Energy 679kcal/2849kJ; Protein 43.9g; Carbohydrate 75.8g, of which sugars 17g; Fat 23.2g, of which saturates 3.7g; Cholesterol 103mg; Calcium 96mg; Fibre 6.3g; Sodium 1207mg.

Shredded duck and bean thread noodle salad

This refreshing, piquant salad makes a mouthwatering first course or light meal. The rich flavour of duck is offset by the addition of fresh, raw vegetables and zesty dressing.

SERVES 4

30ml/2 tbsp rice wine
10ml/2 tsp finely grated fresh root ginger
60ml/4 tbsp soy sauce
15ml/1 tbsp sesame oil
15ml/1 tbsp clear honey
10ml/2 tsp Chinese five-spice powder
4 duck breasts
toasted sesame seeds, to sprinkle

FOR THE NOODLES

150g/5oz bean thread noodles
a handful of coriander (cilantro) leaves
1 red (bell) pepper, seeded and finely sliced
4 spring onions (scallions), finely sliced
50g/2oz mixed salad leaves

FOR THE DRESSING

45ml/3 tbsp light soy sauce
30ml/2 tbsp mirin
10ml/2 tsp golden caster (superfine) sugar
1 garlic clove, crushed
10ml/2 tsp chilli oil

1 Mix together the rice wine, ginger, soy sauce, sesame oil, honey and five-spice powder. Toss over the duck breasts to coat, cover and chill for 3–4 hours.

2 Place a large sheet of foil on a heatproof plate and place the duck breast portions and marinade on top. Fold the foil to enclose the duck and juices and scrunch the edges to seal.

3 Place a trivet in a wok and pour in 5cm/2in water. Bring to the boil and lower the plate on to it. Cover, reduce the heat and steam for 1 hour. Leave to rest for 15 minutes.

4 Meanwhile, place the noodles in a bowl and pour over enough boiling water to cover. Cover and soak for 5–6 minutes. Drain, refresh under cold water and drain again. Transfer to a bowl with the coriander, red pepper, spring onions and salad leaves.

5 Mix together all the dressing ingredients. Remove the skin from the duck breasts and shred the flesh. Divide the noodle salad among four plates and top with the duck. Spoon over the dressing, sprinkle with the sesame seeds and serve immediately.

Nutritional information per portion: Energy 398kcal/1671kJ; Protein 32.8g; Carbohydrate 41.7g, of which sugars 10.8g; Fat 11.6g, of which saturates 2.2g; Cholesterol 165mg; Calcium 40mg; Fibre 1g; Sodium 1688mg.

Chilli noodles

Street stalls and tea houses all over Hong Kong have this on their menus, each establishment having a slightly different version from the next. This recipe is one of the more luxurious.

SERVES 4

400g/14oz dry wheat flour noodles
200g/7oz choi sum
250g/9oz roast pork, thinly sliced
60ml/4 tbsp chilli and garlic sauce
30ml/2 tbsp vegetable or sesame oil
30ml/2 tbsp light soy sauce
30ml/2 tbsp tomato ketchup

VARIATIONS
Spinach, beansprouts, or cos or romaine lettuce can be used instead of choi sum.

1 Cook the noodles in boiling water until tender, following the packet directions for timing. Drain the noodles and put them in a bowl.

2 Cut the choi sum into bitesize pieces. Add to a pan of boiling water and blanch for 1 minute. Drain and mix with the noodles.

3 Halve the roast pork slices if necessary; the aim is to have about 32 pieces of pork in all. Set aside.

4 Mix the chilli and garlic sauce with the oil, soy sauce and tomato ketchup. Add to the noodles and greens and toss lightly to coat. Top with the pork and serve at once.

Nutritional information per portion: Energy 200kcal/070kJ; Protein 18.0g; Carbohydrate 36.6g, of which sugars 7.1g; Fat 3.5g, of which saturates 0.9g; Cholesterol 39mg; Calcium 101mg; Fibre 2.3g; Sodium 975mg.

Fried rice with pork

This is great for using up last night's leftover rice, but for safety's sake, it must have been cooled quickly and kept in the refrigerator, then fried until thoroughly heated.

SERVES 4–6

45ml/3 tbsp vegetable oil
1 onion, chopped
15ml/1 tbsp chopped garlic
115g/4oz pork, cut into small cubes
2 eggs, beaten
500g/2¼lb/4 cups cooked rice
30ml/2 tbsp Thai fish sauce
15ml/1 tbsp dark soy sauce
2.5ml/½ tsp caster (superfine) sugar
4 spring onions (scallions), finely sliced,
     sliced fresh red chillies, and 1 lime,
     cut into wedges, to serve

1 Heat the oil in a wok or large frying pan. Add the chopped onion and garlic and cook for about 2 minutes until softened.

2 Add the pork to the softened onion and garlic. Stir-fry until the pork is cooked through.

3 Add the eggs and cook until scrambled into small lumps.

4 Add the cooked rice and continue to stir and toss, to coat it all with the oil and prevent it from sticking.

5 Add the Thai fish sauce, soy sauce and sugar and mix well. Continue to stir-fry until the rice is thoroughly heated. Spoon into warmed individual bowls and serve with sliced spring onions, chillies and lime wedges.

Nutritional information per portion: Energy 343kcal/1448kJ; Protein 11.2g; Carbohydrate 54.3g, of which sugars 2.2g; Fat 10.6g, of which saturates 2g; Cholesterol 82mg; Calcium 51mg; Fibre 0.6g; Sodium 220mg.

Cantonese fried noodles

Chow mein is popular with the Chinese who believe in turning leftovers into tasty dishes. For this dish, boiled noodles are fried and topped with a savoury sauce containing needs eating up.

SERVES 2–3

225g/8oz lean beef steak or pork fillet
225g/8oz can bamboo shoots, drained
1 leek, trimmed
25g/1oz dried Chinese mushrooms,
   soaked for 30 minutes in 120ml/
   4fl oz/1/2 cup warm water
150g/5oz Chinese leaves (Chinese
   cabbage)
450g/1lb cooked egg noodles
90ml/6 tbsp vegetable oil
30ml/2 tbsp dark soy sauce
15ml/1 tbsp cornflour (cornstarch)
15ml/1 tbsp rice wine or
   medium-dry sherry
5ml/1 tsp sesame oil
5ml/1 tsp caster (superfine) sugar
salt and ground black pepper

1 Slice the meat, bamboo shoots and leek into matchsticks. Drain the mushrooms, saving 90ml/6 tbsp of the water. Discard the stems, then slice the caps finely. Cut the Chinese leaves into 2.5cm/1in pieces.

2 Heat a third of the oil in a wok and fry the noodles. Turn them once, then press them against the base of the wok so they form a flat cake. Cook for 4 minutes, turn the noodle cake over and cook for 3 minutes. Slide on to a heated plate. Keep warm.

3 Heat 30ml/2 tbsp of the oil in the wok. Add the meat and leeks and stir-fry for 15 seconds.

4 Sprinkle over half the soy sauce and then add the bamboo shoots, mushrooms and seasoning. Stir-fry for 1 minute, then transfer to a plate.

5 Heat the remaining oil in the wok and stir-fry the Chinese leaves for 1 minute. Return the meat and vegetables to the wok and stir-fry with the leaves for 30 seconds.

6 Mix the cornflour with the mushroom water. Stir into the wok with the rice wine or sherry, sesame oil, sugar and remaining soy sauce. Cook for 15 seconds to thicken. Serve the noodles immediately with the meat and vegetables piled on top.

Nutritional information per portion: Energy 481kcal/2006kJ; Protein 24.4g; Carbohydrate 28.9g, of which sugars 7.8g; Fat 30.5g, of which saturates 5.7g; Cholesterol 53mg; Calcium 67mg; Fibre 4.4g; Sodium 791mg.

Fried rice with beef

One of the joys of wok cooking is the ease and speed with which a really good meal can be prepared. This delectable beef and rice stir-fry can be on the table in 15 minutes.

SERVES 4

200g/7oz beef steak, chilled
15ml/1 tbsp vegetable oil
2 garlic cloves, finely chopped
1 egg
250g/9oz/2¼ cups cooked jasmine rice
½ medium head broccoli, coarsely chopped
30ml/2 tbsp dark soy sauce
15ml/1 tbsp light soy sauce
5ml/1 tsp palm sugar (jaggery) or light muscovado (brown) sugar
15ml/1 tbsp fish sauce
ground black pepper
chilli sauce, to serve

1 Trim the steak and cut into very thin strips with a sharp knife.

2 Heat the vegetable oil in a wok and cook the garlic over a low to medium heat until golden brown. Do not let it burn. Increase the heat to high, add the steak and stir-fry for 2 minutes.

3 Move the beef to the edges of the wok. Break the egg into the centre.

4 When the egg starts to set, stir-fry it with the meat. Add the rice and toss all the contents of the wok together, scraping up any residue left on the base and mixing it in. Then add the broccoli, soy sauces, sugar and fish sauce and stir-fry for 2 minutes more.

5 Season to taste with pepper and serve immediately, in individual bowls, with chilli sauce.

Nutritional information per portion: Energy 385kcal/1606kJ; Protein 20.7g; Carbohydrate 52.7g, of which sugars 2.5g; Fat 9.8g, of which saturates 2.8g; Cholesterol 81mg; Calcium 59mg; Fibre 1.6g; Sodium 590mg.

Cantonese fried rice

There are many recipes for fried rice, but the Cantonese are past masters at transforming what is basically a humble dish devised to use up yesterday's leftover rice into one fit for emperors.

SERVES 4

600g/1lb 6oz/5¼ cups cooked cold rice
60ml/4 tbsp vegetable oil
½ large onion, chopped
3 eggs
100g/3¾oz lean cooked ham, cubed
100g/3¾oz raw, shelled prawns (shrimp)
50g/2oz canned crab meat
50g/2oz frozen peas
2 spring onions (scallions),
    trimmed and finely sliced
30ml/2 tbsp light soy sauce
½ tsp sugar
ground black pepper
sliced cucumber and chilli sauce, to serve

1 If the rice has been in the refrigerator, rake it with a fork to loosen up the grains.

2 Heat the oil in a wok or heavy pan and fry the onion until soft, but not brown. Push to one side and crack in the eggs. Cook until set, cutting them up roughly with a spatula.

3 Push the eggs to one side and add the ham, prawns and crab meat.

4 Stir-fry for 2 minutes, then add the rice and stir vigorously until heated through. Mix in the peas, spring onions, soy sauce, sugar and black pepper. Serve with cucumber and chilli sauce.

Nutritional information per portion: Energy 437kcal/1837kJ; Protein 20.4g; Carbohydrate 51g, of which sugars 2.3g; Fat 18.4g, of which saturates 3.3g, Cholesterol 211mg, Calcium 84mg, Fibre 1.1g, Sodium 1025mg.

Mixed seafood hor fun

Hor fun is the Cantonese name for stir-fried rice noodles, a popular hawker staple as well as a restaurant dish when enriched with choice ingredients such as beef and prawns.

SERVES 4

150g/5oz rice noodles
8 raw tiger prawns (jumbo shrimp)
30ml/2 tbsp vegetable oil
1/2 large onion, sliced
100g/3³/₄oz squid rings
100g/3³/₄oz/scant 1/2 cup beansprouts
30ml/2 tbsp oyster sauce
2.5ml/1/2 tsp ground black pepper
150ml/1/4 pint/²/₃ cup water or
   fish stock
fresh or pickled chillies, to serve

1 Bring a pan of water to the boil and cook the rice noodles according to the packet instructions or until soft. Taste a strand to check. Drain and set aside.

2 Shell and de-vein the prawns by making a deep slit down the back. This will also make them curl up nicely.

3 Heat the oil in a wok or frying pan and fry the onion until soft. Add the prawns and squid and stir-fry for 2 minutes. Add the beansprouts, noodles, oyster sauce and pepper and stir to toss well. Add the water or stock and let it bubble and reduce. As soon as the sauce is thick, serve the noodles with fresh or pickled chillies.

Nutritional information per portion: Energy 259Kcal/1084kJ; Protein 15.3g; Carbohydrate 34g, of which sugars 2.6g; Fat 6.4g, of which saturates 0.8g; Cholesterol 154mg; Calcium 53mg; Fibre 0.5g; Sodium 251mg.

Lobster noodles

This dish is sure to impress gourmet taste buds. Chinese restaurants present it with great fanfare, with the lobster sitting in all its pink-shelled glory on top of the cooked noodles.

SERVES 4

1 large live or freshly cooked
   lobster, about 1kg/2¼lb
400g/14oz dried egg noodles
30ml/2 tbsp vegetable oil
15ml/1 tbsp crushed garlic
100g/3¾oz/½ cup beansprouts
200ml/7fl oz/scant 1 cup water
30ml/2 tbsp oyster sauce
5ml/1 tsp ground black pepper
30ml/2 tbsp sesame oil

1 If the lobster is live, place it in a plastic bag and put it in the freezer for 5–7 hours. Bring a large pan of water to the boil, add the lobster and cook for 10 minutes or until the shell has turned scarlet. Remove and set aside to cool. Cook the noodles according to the packet instructions. Drain and set aside.

2 When the lobster has cooled slightly, use a sharp knife to cut off the head and the tip of the tail. Rinse and set aside for the garnish. Twist off the claws and set aside. Using a sharp pair of poultry shears, cut down the shell from the top to the tail. Remove the lobster meat, and slice it into rounds. Remove the meat from the claws and legs. Set all the lobster meat aside.

3 Heat the oil in a wok and fry the garlic for 40 seconds. Add the beansprouts and stir-fry for 2 minutes. Add the noodles, water, oyster sauce, black pepper and sesame oil and cook, stirring, for 2 minutes. Add the lobster slices and toss lightly. Arrange on a large oval plate, making sure that the lobster pieces are fairly prominent. Decorate with the lobster head and tail.

Nutritional information per portion: Energy 501kcal/2110kJ; Protein 29.9g; Carbohydrate 56.9g, of which sugars 4g; Fat 18.8g, of which saturates 3.5g; Cholesterol 123mg; Calcium 83mg; Fibre 2.6g; Sodium 559mg.

Fish & shellfish

Synonymous with Chinese cuisine, the delicate flavours of fish and shellfish are the perfect foil for the robust and aromatic ingredients found in the Orient. Whole fish, such as Steamed Fish with Five Willow Sauce, make a dramatic centrepiece to a traditional banquet, and elegant shellfish dishes, like Scallops with Black Bean Sauce, look stunning but take only moments to prepare.

Steamed fish with five willow sauce

A fish kettle will come in useful for this recipe. Carp is traditionally used, but any chunky fish that can be cooked whole such as salmon or sea bream can be given this treatment. Make sure you have a suitable large platter for serving this spectacular dish.

SERVES 4

1–2 carp or similar whole fish, total weight
   about 1kg/2¹/₄lb, cleaned and scaled
2.5cm/1in piece fresh root ginger, peeled
   and thinly sliced
4 spring onions (scallions), cut into
   thin strips
2.5ml/¹/₂ tsp salt

FOR THE FIVE WILLOW SAUCE
375g/13oz jar chow chow (Chinese sweet
   mixed pickles)

300ml/¹/₂ pint/1¹/₄ cups water
30ml/2 tbsp rice vinegar
25ml/1¹/₂ tbsp sugar
25ml/1¹/₂ tbsp cornflour (cornstarch)
15ml/1 tbsp light soy sauce
15ml/1 tbsp rice wine or
   medium-dry sherry
1 small green (bell) pepper, seeded and diced
1 carrot, peeled and cut
   into matchsticks
1 tomato, peeled, seeded and diced

1 Rinse the fish inside and out. Dry with kitchen paper. Create a support for each fish by placing a broad strip of oiled foil on the work surface. Place the fish on the foil. Mix the ginger, spring onions and salt, then tuck the mixture into the body cavity.

2 Fold up one or two pieces of foil to make a long wide strip. You will need one for each fish. Place the fish on the foil and then lift the fish on to the trivet. Lower the trivet into the fish kettle and tuck the ends of the foil over the fish.

3 Pour boiling water into the fish kettle to a depth of 2.5cm/1in. Bring to a full rolling boil, then lower the heat and cook the fish until the flesh flakes, topping up the kettle with boiling water as necessary.

4 Meanwhile, prepare the sauce. Put the chow chow into a sieve (strainer) placed over a bowl and reserve the liquid. Cut each of the sweet pickles in half. Pour 250ml/8fl oz/1 cup of the water into a pan and bring to the boil. Add the vinegar and sugar and stir until dissolved.

5 In a small bowl, mix the cornflour to a paste with the remaining water. Stir in the soy sauce and rice wine or sherry.

6 Add the mixture to the sauce and bring to the boil, stirring until it thickens and becomes glossy. Add all the vegetables, the chopped pickles and the pickle liquid and cook over a gentle heat for 2 minutes.

7 Using the foil strips as a support, carefully transfer the cooked fish to a platter, then ease the foil away. Spoon the warm sauce over the fish and serve.

Nutritional information per portion: Energy 321kcal/1350kJ; Protein 45.3g; Carbohydrate 8.1g, of which sugars 6.6g; Fat 12.2g, of which saturates 2.4g; Cholesterol 168mg; Calcium 150mg; Fibre 2.6g; Sodium 784mg.

Braised grouper in black bean sauce

Grouper is one of the most desirable fish on account of its rich flavour and meaty texture.
Traditionally, fish is braised whole, head and all, and only the most inedible fins are removed.

SERVES 4

1 grouper, about 450g/1lb
vegetable oil, for deep-frying
30ml/2 tbsp chopped spring onions
     (scallions) and fresh coriander
     (cilantro) sprigs, to garnish

FOR THE SAUCE

30ml/2 tbsp black bean sauce
15ml/1 tbsp oyster sauce
10ml/2 tsp garlic purée
10g/2 tsp ginger purée
5ml/1 tsp sugar
2.5ml/½ tsp ground black pepper
30ml/2 tbsp sesame oil
60ml/4 tbsp rice wine
15ml/1 tbsp cornflour (cornstarch), to
     thicken (optional)

1 Gut and clean the fish but leave the head on. Trim off the fins with scissors and cut off half the tail if it protrudes too much from the pan you intend on cooking it in. Heat enough oil for deep-frying in a wok or large pan and fry the grouper until golden brown.

2 Blend all the sauce ingredients with 400ml/14fl oz/1⅔ cups water and mix well. Bring to the boil in a wok or deep pan and cook for 2 minutes. Add the whole fish and simmer, uncovered, for 10 minutes.

3 Spoon the sauce over the fish from time to time as it cooks, but do not turn the fish over as it might break.

4 Serve the fish hot, garnished with coriander. If you wish to thicken the sauce, mix the cornflour with a little water and stir it into the sauce for the last 2 minutes of cooking.

Nutritional information per portion: Energy 173kcal/727kJ; Protein 14.5g; Carbohydrate 8.8g, of which sugars 5.2g; Fat 7.4g, of which saturates 1.2g; Cholesterol 26mg; Calcium 38mg; Fibre 0.2g; Sodium 274mg.

Chinese-style steamed fish

This is the classic Chinese way of cooking whole fish, with garlic, spring onions, ginger and black beans. The fish makes a delectable and impressive centrepiece for a Chinese meal.

SERVES 4–6

2 sea bass, grey mullet or trout,
   each weighing about 675–800g/
   1½–1¾lb, cleaned
30ml/2 tbsp finely shredded
   fresh root ginger
4 garlic cloves, thinly sliced
25ml/1½ tbsp salted black beans
2.5ml/½ tsp sugar
30ml/2 tbsp rice wine
30ml/2 tbsp light soy sauce
4–6 spring onions (scallions), finely
   shredded or sliced diagonally
10ml/2 tsp sesame oil

1 Wash the fish under cold running water, then pat them dry on kitchen paper. Slash three or four deep cross shapes on each side of each fish. Place a little ginger and garlic inside the cavity of each fish and then lay them on a plate or dish that will fit inside a large steamer.

2 Mash half the black beans with the sugar in a small bowl and then stir in the remaining whole beans. Rub the bean mixture into the fish, especially into the slashes, then sprinkle the remaining ginger and garlic over the top. Cover the fish with clear film (plastic wrap) and chill for 30 minutes.

3 Place the steamer over a pan of simmering water. Sprinkle the rice wine and half the soy sauce over the fish, and steam them for 15–20 minutes until cooked through.

4 Sprinkle the fish with the remaining soy sauce and the sesame oil, then garnish with the spring onions. Serve immediately.

Nutritional information per portion: Energy 260kcal/1095kJ; Protein 41.9g; Carbohydrate 1.5g, of which sugars 1g; Fat 9.1g, of which saturates 2g; Cholesterol 171mg; Calcium 69mg; Fibre 0.2g; Sodium 512mg.

Sweet and sour fish

When fish such as red mullet or snapper is deep-fried in oil the skin becomes crisp, while the flesh inside remains moist and juicy. The sweet and sour sauce perfectly complements the fish.

SERVES 4–6

1 large or 2 medium fish, such as snapper
   or mullet, cleaned, with heads removed
20ml/4 tsp cornflour (cornstarch)
120ml/4fl oz/½ cup vegetable oil
15ml/1 tbsp chopped garlic
15ml/1 tbsp chopped fresh root ginger
30ml/2 tbsp chopped shallots
225g/8oz cherry tomatoes
30ml/2 tbsp red wine vinegar
30ml/2 tbsp sugar
30ml/2 tbsp tomato ketchup
15ml/1 tbsp fish sauce
45ml/3 tbsp water
salt and ground black pepper
shredded spring onions (scallions),
   to garnish

1 Rinse and dry the fish. Score the skin diagonally on both sides, then coat the fish lightly all over with 15ml/1 tbsp of the cornflour. Heat the oil in a wok. Add the fish and cook over a medium heat for 6–7 minutes. Turn the fish over and cook for 6–7 minutes more, until it is crisp and brown.

2 Remove the fish and place on a large platter. Pour off all but 30ml/2 tbsp of the oil from the wok and reheat. Add the garlic, ginger and shallots and cook, stirring occasionally, for 4 minutes, until golden. Add the tomatoes and cook until they burst open. Stir in the vinegar, sugar, tomato ketchup and fish sauce. Lower the heat and simmer for 2 minutes.

3 Mix the remaining cornflour with the water. Stir into the sauce to thicken. Pour the sauce over the fish, garnish with shredded spring onions and serve.

Nutritional information per portion: Energy 245kcal/1023kJ; Protein 16.2g; Carbohydrate 14.8g, of which sugars 10.6g; Fat 13.8g, of which saturates 1.6g; Cholesterol 38mg; Calcium 27mg; Fibre 1.1g; Sodium 138mg.

Grey mullet with pork

The combination of fish and pork may sound unusual but the mix of textures and the subtle Chinese flavourings make this a wonderful main course dish that requires little effort.

SERVES 4

1 grey mullet, about 900g/2lb, gutted
    and cleaned
50g/2oz lean pork
3 dried Chinese mushrooms, soaked in
    hot water until soft
2.5ml/¹/₂ tsp cornflour (cornstarch)
30ml/2 tbsp light soy sauce
15ml/1 tbsp vegetable oil
15ml/1 tbsp finely shredded fresh
    root ginger
15ml/1 tbsp shredded spring onion
    (scallion)
salt and ground black pepper
sliced spring onions (scallions), to garnish
rice, to serve

1 Make four diagonal cuts on both sides of the fish and rub with salt; place the fish on a heatproof serving dish. Cut the pork into thin strips. Place in a bowl.

2 Drain the mushrooms, remove and discard the stalks and slice the caps thinly. Add the mushrooms to the pork, with the cornflour and half the soy sauce. Stir in 5ml/1tsp of the oil and a grinding of black pepper. Arrange the mixture along the length of the fish. Sprinkle the ginger over the top.

3 Cover the fish loosely with foil. Place the dish on a metal trivet in a roasting pan with 5cm/2in boiling water, cover and steam for 15 minutes. Test the fish by pressing the flesh gently. If it comes away from the bone with a slight resistance, the fish is cooked.

4 Heat the remaining oil in a small pan and fry the shredded spring onion for a few seconds, then pour it over the fish. Drizzle with the remaining soy sauce, garnish with sliced spring onions and serve immediately with rice.

Nutritional information per portion: Energy 228kcal/960kJ; Protein 34.7g; Carbohydrate 0.7g, of which sugars 0.6g; Fat 9.8g, of which saturates 2.3g; Cholesterol 62mg; Calcium 46mg; Fibre 0.1g; Sodium 647mg.

Mackerel with shiitake mushrooms and black beans

Earthy-tasting shiitake mushrooms, zesty fresh ginger and pungent salted black beans are the perfect partners for the robustly flavoured mackerel fillets used in this recipe.

SERVES 4

8 x 115g/4oz mackerel fillets

20 dried Chinese mushrooms

15ml/1 tbsp finely julienned fresh root ginger

3 star anise

45ml/3 tbsp dark soy sauce

15ml/1 tbsp rice wine

15ml/1 tbsp salted black beans

6 spring onions (scallions), finely shredded

30ml/2 tbsp sunflower oil

5ml/1 tsp sesame oil

4 garlic cloves, very thinly sliced

sliced cucumber and steamed basmati rice, to serve

1 Divide the mackerel fillets between two oiled heatproof plates, with the skin-side up. Make 3–4 diagonal slits in each one, then set aside.

2 Place the mushrooms in a large bowl and pour over enough boiling water to cover. Leave to soak for 20–25 minutes. Drain, reserving the soaking liquid, discard the stems and slice the caps thinly.

3 Place a trivet in a large wok and pour in 5cm/2in of the mushroom liquid (top up with water if necessary). Add half the ginger and the star anise.

4 Push the remaining ginger strips into the slits in the fish and sprinkle over the mushrooms. Bring the liquid in the wok to the boil and lower one of the plates on to the trivet. Cover the wok, reduce the heat and steam for 10–12 minutes, or until the mackerel is cooked through. Remove the plate from the wok and repeat with the second plate of fish, replenishing the liquid in the wok if necessary.

5 Transfer the steamed fish to a large serving platter. Ladle 105ml/7 tbsp of the steaming liquid into a clean wok with the soy sauce, wine and black beans, place over a gentle heat and bring to a simmer. Spoon over the fish and sprinkle over the spring onions.

6 Wipe out the wok with a piece of kitchen paper and place the wok over a medium heat. Add the oils and garlic and stir-fry for a few minutes until lightly golden. Pour over the fish and serve immediately with sliced cucumber and steamed basmati rice.

Nutritional information per portion: Energy 693kcal/2872kJ; Protein 45.5g; Carbohydrate 1.9g, of which sugars 0.5g; Fat 55.9g, of which saturates 10.4g; Cholesterol 128mg; Calcium 35mg; Fibre 0.6g; Sodium 152mg.

Beansprouts with salt fish

This simple peasant dish has been elevated to gourmet status. If you can find them, use salted fillets of snapper or a tropical fish called threadfin (ma yeow yu in Cantonese).

SERVES 4

100g/3³/₄oz salt fish fillet
60ml/4 tbsp vegetable oil
600g/1lb 6oz/2¹/₃ cups beansprouts
2 spring onions (scallions)
30ml/2 tbsp crushed garlic
15ml/1 tbsp light soy sauce

COOK'S TIP
Sprout your own soya beans, if possible. If you do buy the sprouts, however, look for ones with large heads, as these are the healthiest option.

1 Cut the salt fish into small chunks. Heat the oil in a wok and fry the pieces of salt fish until fragrant and slightly brittle. With a slotted spoon, transfer them to a board. Let them cool slightly, then shred them roughly.

2 Wash the beansprouts, drain them thoroughly and remove any green husks. Cut the spring onions into 5cm/2in lengths.

3 Pour off all but 30ml/2 tbsp of the oil from the wok. Heat the remaining oil and stir-fry the garlic until golden brown. Add the beansprouts and salt fish and stir-fry rapidly for 2 minutes.

4 Add the spring onions and stir-fry for 1 minute. Drizzle over the soy sauce and stir for 1 further minute. Transfer to four warmed bowls and serve immediately.

Nutritional information per portion: Energy 185kcal/772kJ; Protein 13.2g; Carbohydrate 6.5g, of which sugars 3.7g; Fat 12.1g, of which saturates 1.5g; Cholesterol 0mg; Calcium 68mg; Fibre 2.3g; Sodium 2157mg.

Raw fish salad

To celebrate the lunar New Year, Chinese families get together to eat special dishes such as this salad, yu sheng, which all the diners must help to mix with their chopsticks.

SERVES 4–6

175g/6oz fresh tuna or salmon, finely sliced
115g/4oz white fish fillet, finely sliced
25g/1oz fresh root ginger, finely chopped
2 garlic cloves, crushed
juice of 2 limes
225g/8oz mooli (daikon)
2 carrots
1 small cucumber, peeled and seeded
4 spring onions (scallions), trimmed
1 pomelo, segmented and sliced
4 fresh kaffir lime leaves, cut into ribbons
50g/2oz preserved sweet melon, sliced
ground black pepper
30ml/2 tbsp roasted peanuts, crushed

FOR THE DRESSING

30ml/2 tbsp sesame oil
15ml/1 tbsp light soy sauce
15ml/1 tbsp red vinegar
30ml/2 tbsp sour plum sauce
2 garlic cloves, crushed
10ml/2 tsp caster (superfine) sugar

1 In a shallow, non-metallic dish, toss the slices of fish with the ginger, garlic and lime juice.

2 Season the fish with black pepper and set aside for at least 30 minutes to marinate.

3 Cut the mooli, carrots, cucumber and spring onions into fine julienne strips, and place in a large bowl with the sliced pomelo and lime leaves.

4 Add the pieces of preserved melon to the bowl. Toss everything together well to ensure an even distribution of ingredients.

5 In a small mixing bowl stir together all of the the ingredients for the dressing, adjusting the sweet and sour balance to taste.

6 Place the marinated slices of fish on top of the vegetables in the bowl. Pour the dressing over the top and sprinkle liberally with the roasted peanuts.

7 To serve, place the bowl in the middle of the table and get everyone to toss the salad with their chopsticks until all of the ingredients are well combined and everything is generously coated with the dressing.

Nutritional information per portion: Energy 126kcal/528kJ; Protein 13.2g; Carbohydrate 6.5g, of which sugars 6.4g; Fat 5.4g, of which saturates 1g; Cholesterol 22mg; Calcium 36mg; Fibre 1.3g; Sodium 222mg.

Steamed fish skewers on herbed rice noodles

In this recipe, succulent fillets of fresh trout are marinated in a tangy citrus spice blend, then skewered and steamed before serving on a bed of fragrant herb noodles.

SERVES 4

4 trout fillets, skinned
2.5ml/¹/₂ tsp turmeric
15ml/1 tbsp mild curry paste
juice of 2 lemons
15ml/1 tbsp sunflower oil
salt and ground black pepper
45ml/3 tbsp chilli-roasted peanuts,
   roughly chopped, and chopped fresh mint,
   to garnish

FOR THE NOODLES

300g/11oz rice noodles
15ml/1 tbsp sunflower oil
1 red chilli, seeded and finely sliced
4 spring onions (scallions),
   cut into slivers
60ml/4 tbsp roughly chopped fresh mint
60ml/4 tbsp roughly chopped
   fresh sweet basil

1 Trim each fillet and place in a large bowl. Mix together the turmeric, curry paste, lemon juice and oil and pour over the fish. Season with salt and black pepper and toss to mix well.

2 Place the rice noodles in a bowl and pour over enough boiling water to cover. Leave to soak for 3–4 minutes and then drain. Refresh in cold water, drain and set aside.

3 Thread 2 bamboo skewers through each trout fillet and arrange in two tiers of a bamboo steamer lined with baking parchment.

4 Cover the steamer and place over a wok of simmering water (making sure the water doesn't touch the steamer). Steam the fish skewers for 5–6 minutes, or until the fish is just cooked through.

5 Meanwhile, in a clean wok heat the oil. Add the chilli, spring onions and drained noodles and stir-fry for about 2 minutes and then stir in the chopped herbs. Season with salt and ground black pepper and divide among four bowls or plates.

6 Top each bowl of noodles with a steamed fish skewer and sprinkle over the chilli-roasted peanuts. Garnish with chopped mint and serve immediately.

Nutritional information per portion: Energy 159kcal/664kJ; Protein 13.5g; Carbohydrate 10.6g, of which sugars 0.4g; Fat 6.9g, of which saturates 1.7g; Cholesterol 157mg; Calcium 46mg; Fibre 0g; Sodium 526mg.

Three sea flavours stir-fry

The delectable and luxurious combination of scallops, monkfish and tiger prawns is enhanced with the simple and refreshing flavours of fresh root ginger and spring onions.

SERVES 4

4 large scallops, with the corals
225g/8oz firm white fish fillet, such as
    monkfish or cod
115g/4oz raw tiger prawns (jumbo shrimp)
300ml/½ pint/1¼ cups fish stock
15ml/1 tbsp vegetable oil
2 garlic cloves, coarsely chopped
5cm/2in piece of fresh root ginger,
    thinly sliced
8 spring onions (scallions), cut into
    4 cm/1½ in pieces
30ml/2 tbsp dry white wine
5ml/1 tsp cornflour (cornstarch)
15ml/1 tbsp cold water
salt and ground white pepper
noodles or rice, to serve

1 Separate the corals and slice each scallop in half horizontally. Cut the fish fillet into bitesize chunks. Peel and devein the prawns.

2 Bring the fish stock to the boil in a pan. Add the seafood, lower the heat and poach gently for 1–2 minutes until the fish, scallops and corals are just firm and the prawns have turned pink. Drain the seafood, reserving about 60ml/4 tbsp of the stock.

3 Heat the oil in a wok. Stir-fry the garlic, ginger and spring onions for a few seconds. Add the seafood and wine. Stir-fry for 1 minute, then add the reserved stock and simmer for 2 minutes.

4 Mix the cornflour to a paste with the water. Add the mixture to the wok and cook, stirring gently just until the sauce thickens. Season the stir-fry with salt and pepper to taste. Serve at once, with noodles or rice.

Nutritional information per portion: Energy 147kcal/620kJ; Protein 23g; Carbohydrate 4g, of which sugars 1g; Fat 5g, of which saturates 1g; Cholesterol 80mg; Calcium 47mg; Fibre 0.0g; Sodium 229mg

Noodle pancake with prawns, scallops and squid

In dishes of Chinese origin, egg noodles are used instead of rice noodles. For this popular dish, the Chinese prefer to use thin Shanghai-style noodles, which are available in Asian markets.

SERVES 4

225g/8oz fresh egg noodles

60–75ml/4–5 tbsp vegetable oil, plus
    extra for brushing

4cm/1½in fresh root ginger, peeled and
    cut into matchsticks

4 spring onions (scallions), trimmed and
    cut into bitesize pieces

1 carrot, peeled and thinly sliced

8 scallops, halved if large

8 baby squid, cut in half lengthways

8 tiger prawns (jumbo shrimp), shelled
    and deveined

30ml/2 tbsp nuoc mam

45ml/3 tbsp soy sauce

5ml/1 tsp sugar

ground black pepper

coriander (cilantro) leaves, to garnish

fish sauce, to serve

1 Cook the noodles according to their packet instructions. Drain and spread them out into a wide, thick pancake on an oiled plate. Allow to dry slightly.

2 Heat 30ml/2 tbsp of the oil in a non-stick pan. Slide the noodle pancake into the pan and cook over a medium heat until crisp. Add 15ml/ 1 tbsp oil to the pan, flip the pancake over and crisp the other side.

3 Meanwhile, heat a wok and add the remaining oil. Add the ginger and spring onions, and cook until fragrant.

4 Add the carrot, and stir-fry the mixture for 1–2 minutes.

5 Add the scallops, squid and prawns, moving them around the wok, so that they sear while cooking.

6 Stir in the nuoc mam, soy sauce and sugar and season well with black pepper.

7 Transfer the crispy noodle pancake to a serving dish and spread the seafood on top. Garnish with coriander and serve immediately.

Nutritional information per portion: Energy 807kcal/3401kJ; Protein 83g; Carbohydrate 53g, of which sugars 48g; Fat 31g, of which saturates 5g; Cholesterol 97.5mg; Calcium 110mg; Fibre 2.3g; Sodium 160mg

Monkfish and scallop skewers

Luxurious and delicately flavoured, monkfish makes any meal special. This impressive recipe uses lemon grass stalks as fragrant skewers that imbue the seafood with a subtle citrus flavour.

SERVES 4

450g/1lb monkfish fillet
8 lemon grass stalks
30ml/2 tbsp fresh lemon juice
15ml/1 tbsp olive oil
15ml/1 tbsp coriander (cilantro), finely
    chopped
2.5ml/¹/₂ tsp salt
a large pinch of ground black pepper
12 large scallops, halved crossways
fresh coriander leaves, to garnish
rice, to serve

1 Remove any membrane from the monkfish, then cut into 16 large chunks. Remove the outer leaves from the lemon grass to leave thin rigid stalks. Chop the tender parts of the lemon grass leaves finely and place in a bowl. Stir in the lemon juice, oil, chopped coriander, salt and pepper.

2 Thread the fish and scallop chunks alternately on the eight lemon grass stalks. Arrange the skewers of fish and shellfish in a shallow dish and pour over the marinade.

3 Cover and leave in a cool place for 1 hour, turning occasionally. Transfer the skewers to a heatproof dish or bamboo steamer, cover and steam over boiling water for 10 minutes until just cooked. Garnish with coriander and serve with rice and the cooking juice poured over.

Nutritional information per portion: Energy 150kcal/635kJ; Protein 26g; Carbohydrate 1g, of which sugars 0g; Fat 5g, of which saturates 1g; Cholesterol 32mg; Calcium 21mg; Fibre 0.0g; Sodium 331mg

Squid with broccoli

The slightly chewy squid contrasts beautifully with the crisp crunch of the broccoli to give this dish the perfect combination of textures so beloved by the Chinese.

SERVES 4

300ml/½ pint/1¼ cups fish stock
350g/12oz prepared squid, cut into
   large pieces
225g/8oz broccoli
15ml/1 tbsp vegetable oil
2 garlic cloves, finely chopped
15ml/1 tbsp rice wine or dry sherry
10ml/2 tsp cornflour (cornstarch)
2.5ml/½ tsp caster (superfine) sugar
45ml/3 tbsp cold water
15ml/1 tbsp oyster sauce
2.5ml/½ tsp sesame oil
noodles, to serve

1 Bring the fish stock to the boil in a wok or pan. Add the squid pieces and cook for 2 minutes over a medium heat until they are tender and have curled. Drain the squid pieces and set aside until required.

2 Trim the broccoli and cut it into small florets. Bring a pan of salted water to the boil, add the broccoli and cook for 2 minutes until tender. Drain thoroughly.

3 Heat the vegetable oil in a wok or non-stick frying pan. When the oil is hot, add the garlic, stir fry for a few seconds, then add the squid, broccoli and wine or sherry. Stir-fry the mixture over a medium heat for about 2 minutes.

4 Mix the cornflour and sugar to a paste with the water. Stir the mixture into the wok or pan, with the oyster sauce. Cook, stirring, until the sauce thickens slightly. Just before serving, stir in the sesame oil. Serve with noodles.

Nutritional information per portion: Energy 143kcal/602kJ; Protein 18.2g; Carbohydrate 5.4g, of which sugars 3.6g; Fat 5.6g, of which saturates 0.9g; Cholesterol 253mg; Calcium 32mg; Fibre 1g; Sodium 124mg.

Stir-fried squid with ginger

There's an ancient belief that a well-loved wok holds the memory of all the dishes that have ever been cooked in it. Give yours something to remember by introducing it to this classic.

SERVES 2

4 ready-prepared baby squid, total weight about 250g/9oz
15ml/1 tbsp vegetable oil
2 garlic cloves, finely chopped
30ml/2 tbsp soy sauce
2.5cm/1in piece fresh root ginger, peeled and finely chopped
juice of 1/2 lemon
5ml/1 tsp sugar
2 spring onions (scallions), chopped
noodles, to serve

1 Rinse the squid well and pat dry with kitchen paper. Cut the bodies into rings and halve the tentacles, if necessary.

2 Heat the oil in a wok or frying pan and cook the garlic until golden brown, but do not let it burn.

3 Add the squid to the wok or frying pan and stir-fry for 30 seconds over a high heat.

4 Add the soy sauce, ginger, lemon juice, sugar and spring onions. Stir-fry for a further 30 seconds. Serve with noodles.

Nutritional information per portion: Energy 165kcal/694kJ; Protein 19.7g; Carbohydrate 4.8g, of which sugars 3.2g; Fat 7.6g, of which saturates 1.2g; Cholesterol 281mg; Calcium 20mg; Fibre 0g; Sodium 1206mg.

Five-spice squid with chilli and black bean sauce

Squid is perfect for stir-frying as it benefits from being cooked quickly. The spicy sauce used in this recipe makes an ideal accompaniment and can be put together very quickly.

SERVES 6

450g/1lb small prepared squid

15ml/1 tbsp vegetable oil

2.5cm/1in piece fresh root ginger, grated

1 garlic clove, crushed

8 spring onions (scallions), cut diagonally into 2.5cm/1in lengths

1 red (bell) pepper, seeded and cut into strips

1 fresh green chilli, thinly sliced

6 mushrooms, sliced

5ml/1 tsp five-spice powder

30ml/2 tbsp black bean sauce

30ml/2 tbsp soy sauce

5ml/1 tsp sugar

15ml/1 tbsp rice wine or dry sherry

1 Rinse the squid and pull away the outer skin. Dry on kitchen paper. Make a lengthways slit down the body of each squid, then open out the body flat. Score the outside of the bodies in a criss-cross pattern with the tip of a sharp knife. Cut the squid into strips.

2 Heat the oil in a wok. When it is hot, stir-fry the squid quickly. Remove the squid from the wok with a slotted spoon and set aside.

3 Add the ginger, garlic, spring onions, red pepper, chilli and mushrooms to the oil in the wok and stir-fry for 2 minutes.

4 Return the partially cooked squid to the wok and stir in the five-spice powder. Stir in the black bean sauce, soy sauce, sugar and rice wine or sherry. Bring to the boil and cook, stirring continuously, for about 1 minute. Serve immediately in warmed bowls.

Nutritional information per portion: Energy 134kcal/562kJ; Protein 15.1g; Carbohydrate 4.8g, of which sugars 3.5g; Fat 6.2g, of which saturates 0.9g; Cholesterol 202mg; Calcium 23mg; Fibre 0.9g; Sodium 956mg.

Salt and pepper prawns

This spicy dish flavoured with chillies, ginger and fried salt and peppercorns is a Cantonese classic and makes a delicious suppertime treat. Serve it with plain boiled rice.

SERVES 3–4

15–18 large raw prawns (shrimp), in the shell, about 450g/1lb
vegetable oil, for deep-frying
1 small onion, finely chopped
2 garlic cloves, crushed
1cm/¹/₂in piece fresh root ginger, peeled and very finely grated
1–2 fresh red chillies, seeded and finely sliced
2.5ml/¹/₂ tsp granulated sugar
3–4 spring onions (scallions), sliced, to garnish

FOR THE FRIED SALT

10ml/2 tsp salt
5ml/1 tsp Sichuan peppercorns

1 Make the fried salt by dry-frying the salt and peppercorns in a frying pan over a medium heat until the peppercorns begin to release their aroma. Cool, then crush with a pestle and mortar.

2 Remove the heads and legs from the prawns. Leave the body shells and the tails in place. Pat the prepared prawns dry with kitchen paper.

3 Heat the oil for deep-frying to 190°C/375°F. Fry the prawns for 1 minute, then drain on kitchen paper.

4 Spoon 30ml/2 tbsp of the hot oil into a large frying pan and reheat. Add the fried salt, with the finely chopped onion, garlic, ginger, chillies and sugar. Toss together for 1 minute.

5 Add the prawns to the pan and toss them over the heat for 1 minute more until they are coated and the shells are impregnated with the seasonings.

6 Serve the prawns at once, garnished with the spring onions.

Nutritional information per portion: Energy 172kcal/717kJ; Protein 20.1g; Carbohydrate 2.7g, of which sugars 2.4g; Fat 9g, of which saturates 1.1g; Cholesterol 219mg; Calcium 97mg; Fibre 0.3g; Sodium 1197mg.

Stir-fried water convolvulus

Water convolvulus is a favourite with the people of southern China. Cooks sometimes add preserved beancurd, yellow bean paste or whole preserved yellow beans, as here.

SERVES 4

400g/14oz water convolvulus
  (swamp cabbage)
30ml/2 tbsp vegetable oil
30ml/2 tbsp chopped garlic
200g/7oz raw prawns
  (shrimp), peeled
30ml/2 tbsp whole preserved
  yellow beans
2 fresh red chillies, seeded and sliced
90ml/6 tbsp water

1 Slice the water convolvulus stalks thinly and pluck off the leaves. Wash in plenty of water as the vegetable is grown in brackish water and mud is sometimes trapped in crevices in the stalks. Drain well and leave to air-dry or pat dry with kitchen paper.

2 Heat the oil in a wok and fry the garlic for 40 seconds, until golden.

3 Add the prawns, yellow beans and chillies to the wok and toss together over the heat for 1 minute.

4 Add the water. Cover the wok with a lid, or improvise and make one from foil. Cook for 3 minutes until the leaves and stalks of the water convolvulus shrink and turn dark green. Turn into a heated bowl and serve immediately.

Nutritional information per portion: Energy 138kcal/574kJ; Protein 12.1g; Carbohydrate 8.6g, of which sugars 5.2g, Fat 6.2g, of which saturates 0.7g, Cholesterol 98mg, Calcium 97mg, Fibre 2.7g, Sodium 104mg.

Gong boa prawns

This pleasantly spicy sweet-and-sour dish makes an excellent midweek supper as it takes only minutes to make. Delicious served with simple noodles or plain boiled rice.

SERVES 4

350g/12oz raw tiger prawns
   (jumbo shrimp)
1/2 cucumber, about 75g/3oz
300ml/1/2 pint/11/4 cups fish stock
15ml/1 tbsp vegetable oil
2.5ml/1/2 tsp crushed dried chillies
1/2 green (bell) pepper, seeded and cut
   into 2.5cm/1in strips
1 small carrot, thinly sliced
30ml/2 tbsp tomato ketchup
45ml/3 tbsp rice vinegar
15ml/1 tbsp caster (superfine) sugar
150ml/1/4 pint/2/3 cup vegetable stock
50g/2oz/1/2 cup drained canned
   pineapple chunks
10ml/2 tsp cornflour (cornstarch)
15ml/1 tbsp cold water
salt

1 Peel and devein the prawns. Rub them gently with 2.5ml/1/2 tsp salt; leave them for a few minutes and then wash and dry thoroughly. Cut the cucumber in half lengthways and scoop out the seeds with a teaspoon. Cut the flesh into 5mm/1/4in crescents.

2 Bring the fish stock to the boil in a large pan. Add the prawns, lower the heat and poach for 2 minutes until they turn pink, then drain and set aside. Heat the oil in a wok over a high heat. Fry the chillies for a few seconds, then add the pepper strips and carrot slices and stir-fry for 1 minute.

3 Mix together the tomato ketchup, vinegar, sugar and vegetable stock, with 1.5ml/1/4 tsp salt. Pour into the pan and stir-fry for 3 minutes more.

4 Add the prawns, cucumber and pineapple and cook for 2 minutes more. Mix the cornflour to a paste with the water. Add the mixture to the pan and cook, stirring constantly, until the sauce thickens. Serve at once.

Nutritional information per portion: Energy 147kcal/617kJ; Protein 16.3g; Carbohydrate 13.2g, of which sugars 10.7g; Fat 3.5g, of which saturates 0.5g; Cholesterol 171mg; Calcium 88mg; Fibre 1.1g; Sodium 296mg.

Chinese broccoli with king prawns

Chinese broccoli (kai lan) comes from the same family as broccoli, and it is a favourite among the Chinese. The leaves are dark green and the thick stalks have a nice crunch.

SERVES 2

200g/7oz Chinese broccoli (kai lan)

200g/7oz king or tiger prawns (jumbo shrimp)

2 garlic cloves, crushed

30ml/2 tbsp vegetable oil

30g/2 tbsp oyster sauce

1/2 tsp ground black pepper

90ml/3fl oz/1/4 cup water

1 Trim off the hard ends of the Chinese broccoli stalks and slice into diagonal pieces about 7.5cm/3in long. Wash and dry.

2 Shell the prawns, wash and pat dry. Remove the dark veins by making a slit down the back of each prawn.

3 Heat the oil in a wok or large, heavy pan until it is smoking and throw in the kai lan and garlic. Stir-fry for 2 minutes, then add the prawns.

4 Continue to stir-fry for 2 minutes while adding the oyster sauce, pepper and water.

5 When the leaves wilt a little, the vegetables are done. Serve at once.

Nutritional information per portion: Energy 225Kcal/939kJ; Protein 22.3g; Carbohydrate 6.1g, of which sugars 5.7g; Fat 12.5g, of which saturates 1.6g; Cholesterol 195mg; Calcium 137mg; Fibre 2.8g; Sodium 443mg.

Steamed scallops with ginger

It helps to have two woks when making this dish. If you are not doubly blessed, borrow an extra one from a friend, or use a large, heavy pan with a trivet for steaming the second plate of scallops. Take care not to overcook the tender seafood.

SERVES 4

24 king scallops in their shells, cleaned

15ml/1 tbsp very finely shredded fresh
   root ginger

5ml/1 tsp very finely chopped garlic

1 large fresh red chilli, seeded and
   very finely chopped

15ml/1 tbsp light soy sauce

15ml/1 tbsp rice wine

a few drops of sesame oil

2–3 spring onions (scallions), very
   finely shredded

15ml/1 tbsp very finely chopped
   fresh chives

noodles, to serve

1 Remove the scallops from their shells, then remove the membrane and hard white muscle from each one. Arrange the scallops on two plates. Rinse the shells, dry and set aside.

2 Fill two woks with 5cm/2in water and place a trivet in the base of each one. Bring to the boil.

3 Mix together the ginger, garlic, chilli, soy sauce, rice wine, sesame oil, spring onions and chives. Spoon over the scallops. Lower a plate into each wok. Turn the heat to low, cover and steam for 10–12 minutes, until tender.

4 Divide the scallops among the reserved shells. Serve with noodles.

Nutritional information per portion: Energy 167kcal/708kJ; Protein 29.8g; Carbohydrate 7g, of which sugars 2.6g; Fat 2g, of which saturates 0.6g; Cholesterol 59mg; Calcium 53mg; Fibre 0.8g; Sodium 496mg.

Scallops with **black bean sauce**

When scallops are fresh, they taste exquisite when simply steamed in their shells. Here they are served with a little flavoursome sauce made from rice wine, fermented black beans and fresh ginger, which perfectly complements the sweet tender flesh of the scallops.

SERVES 4

8 scallops, preferably in the shell
30ml/2 tbsp rice wine
15ml/1 tbsp fermented black beans
15ml/1 tbsp chopped fresh root ginger
2.5ml/¹/₂ tsp sugar
15ml/1 tbsp shredded spring onions
   (scallions)

COOK'S TIPS

• *Save the scallop shells. They can be used as decorative containers in the future.*
• *When black beans are used in any dish, they provide plenty of salt, so there is no need to add any more.*

1 Preheat the oven to 160°C/ 325°F/Gas 3. Spread the scallops on a baking sheet. Heat until they gape. Remove them from the oven.

2 Using a knife, run the blade along the inner surface of the flat shell to cut through the muscle that holds the shells together.

3 Ease the shells apart. Lift off the top shell. Pull out and discard the black intestinal sac and the yellowish frilly membrane.

4 Cut the white scallop and orange coral from the shell and rinse briefly under cold water. Remove and discard the white ligament attached to the scallop flesh.

5 To make the sauce, mix the wine, black beans, ginger and sugar in a shallow dish. Add the scallops and marinate for 30 minutes.

6 Return the scallops and sauce to the shells and steam for 10 minutes. Garnish with spring onions. Serve.

Nutritional information per portion: Energy 75kcal/319kJ; Protein 12.3g; Carbohydrate 3.9g, of which sugars 0.9g; Fat 0.8g, of which saturates 0.2g; Cholesterol 24mg; Calcium 19mg; Fibre 0.3g; Sodium 91mg.

Mussels in chilli and black bean sauce

The large green-shelled mussels from New Zealand are perfect for this delicious dish. Buy the cooked mussels on the half-shell – it is an elegant way to serve them.

SERVES 4

15ml/1 tbsp vegetable oil

2.5cm/1in piece of fresh root ginger,
    finely chopped

2 garlic cloves, finely chopped

1 fresh red chilli, seeded
    and chopped

15ml/1 tbsp black bean sauce

15ml/1 tbsp dry sherry

5ml/1 tsp sugar

5ml/1 tsp sesame oil

10ml/2 tsp dark soy sauce

20 cooked New Zealand green-shelled
    mussels

2 spring onions (scallions),
    1 shredded and 1 cut into fine rings

1 Heat the vegetable oil in a wok. Fry the ginger, garlic and chilli with the black bean sauce for a few seconds, then add the sherry and sugar and cook for 30 seconds, stirring to ensure the sugar is dissolved. Remove the sauce from the heat and stir in the sesame oil and soy sauce.

2 Have ready a bamboo steamer or a pan holding 5cm/2in of simmering water, and fitted with a metal trivet. Place the mussels in a single layer on a heatproof plate that will fit inside the steamer or pan. Spoon over the sauce.

3 Sprinkle all the spring onions over the mussels. Cover the plate tightly with foil and place it on the trivet in the steamer or pan. It should be just above the level of the water. Cover and steam over a high heat for about 10 minutes or until the mussels have heated through. Serve immediately.

Nutritional information per portion: Energy 437kcal/1831kJ; Protein 20.7g; Carbohydrate 34.3g, of which sugars 8.5g; Fat 25.2g, of which saturates 3.8g; Cholesterol 30mg; Calcium 331mg; Fibre 1.5g; Sodium 455mg.

Stir-fried mussels in ginger sauce

Mussels have a great affinity with aromatics like ginger and garlic and, when steeped in a wine sauce, echo the French dish Moules Marinière. Hong Kong chefs sometimes use large clams instead.

SERVES 4

450g/1lb live green-lipped or standard
   mussels, scrubbed and bearded
30ml/2 tbsp vegetable oil
15ml/1 tbsp chopped fresh root ginger
3 garlic cloves, chopped
30ml/2 tbsp rice wine
   or sherry
150ml/¼ pint/⅔ cup water
2.5ml/½ tsp salt
2.5ml/½ tsp ground black pepper

1 Carefully check over the mussels, discarding any that have cracked shells, as well as any that are open and that do not snap shut when tapped on a firm surface.

2 Heat the oil in a wok and fry the ginger and garlic for 40 seconds, until light brown. Add the mussels and stir rapidly over a high heat for 2 minutes, shaking the pan to move the mussels around.

3 Pour in the rice wine or sherry and water. Season with the salt and pepper and toss the mussels over the heat for a further 2–3 minutes, until all of them have opened. Discard any mussels that remain closed. Pile the mussels into a warm serving bowl and serve immediately.

Nutritional information per portion: Energy 97kcal/404kJ; Protein 5.7g; Carbohydrate 2.4g, of which sugars 0.2g; Fat 6.3g, of which saturates 0.8g; Cholesterol 18mg; Calcium 18mg; Fibre 0.3g; Sodium 355mg.

Poultry

Arguably the most famous of all Chinese dishes, Peking Duck with Mandarin Pancakes, is a mainstay of Chinese restaurants around the world. This chapter teaches you how to make this classic dish at home, along with other delicious chicken and duck recipes such as Soy Braised Chicken, Chinese Duck Curry, Lemon and Sesame Chicken and Braised Duck in Aromatic Sauce.

Bang bang chicken

Using toasted sesame paste gives the sauce of this special dish from Sichuan an authentic flavour, although crunchy peanut butter can be used instead. Perfect for parties and ideal for a buffet.

SERVES 4

3 skinless, boneless chicken breasts
1 garlic clove, crushed
2.5ml/¹/₂ tsp black peppercorns
1 small onion, halved
1 cucumber, peeled and cut into thin strips
salt and ground black pepper
60ml/4 tbsp chilli oil

FOR THE SAUCE

45ml/3 tbsp toasted sesame paste
15ml/1 tbsp light soy sauce
15ml/1 tbsp wine vinegar
2 spring onions (scallions), finely chopped
2 garlic cloves, crushed
5 cm/2¹/₂in piece fresh root ginger, cut into matchsticks
15ml/1 tbsp Sichuan peppercorns, dry fried and crushed
5ml/1 tsp light brown sugar

1 Place the chicken in a saucepan. cover with water, add the garlic, peppercorns and onion and bring to the boil. Skim the surface, stir in salt and pepper to taste. Cover and cook for 25 minutes, until the chicken is just tender. Drain, reserving the stock.

2 Make the sauce by mixing the sesame paste with 45ml/3 tbsp of chicken stock, saving the rest for soup.

3 Add the soy sauce, vinegar, spring onions, garlic, ginger and peppercorns to the mixture. Stir in sugar to taste.

4 Spread out the cucumber batons on a platter. Cut the chicken breasts into pieces of about the same size as the cucumber strips and arrange them on top. Pour over the sauce, drizzle on the chilli oil and serve.

Nutritional information per portion: Energy 200kcal/838kJ; Protein 29.5g; Carbohydrate 2.8g, of which sugars 2.4g; Fat 7.9g, of which saturates 1.3g; Cholesterol 79mg; Calcium 89mg; Fibre 1.2g; Sodium 338mg.

Cashew chicken

A popular item on any Chinese restaurant menu, this dish is easy to recreate at home. It is important to have the wok very hot before adding the chicken.

SERVES 4–6

450g/1lb skinless chicken breast fillets
1 red (bell) pepper
2 garlic cloves
4 dried red chillies
30ml/2 tbsp vegetable oil
30ml/2 tbsp oyster sauce
15ml/1 tbsp soy sauce
a pinch of sugar
1 bunch of spring onions (scallions),
    cut into 5cm/2in lengths
175g/6oz/1¹/₂ cups cashews, roasted

1 Trim off any excess fat from the chicken breast fillets. With a sharp knife, cut the chicken into bitesize pieces. Set aside.

2 Halve the red pepper, discard the seeds and membranes, then cut the flesh into 2cm/³/₄in dice. Peel and thinly slice the garlic and chop the dried chillies.

3 Preheat a wok and then drizzle a 'necklace' of oil around the inner rim of the wok, so that it coats the entire inner surface. Swirl the wok to make sure it is even.

4 Add the garlic and dried chillies to the wok and stir-fry over a medium heat until golden. Do not let the garlic burn, otherwise it will taste bitter.

5 Add the chicken breast pieces and stir-fry until cooked through, then add the red pepper. If the mixture is very dry, add a little water. Stir in the oyster sauce, soy sauce and sugar. Add the spring onions and cashew nuts.

6 Stir fry for a further 1–2 minutes, until heated through, and then serve immediately.

Nutritional information per portion: Energy 314kcal/1307kJ; Protein 24.7g; Carbohydrate 10.2g, of which sugars 6.2g; Fat 19.6g, of which saturates 3.7g; Cholesterol 53mg; Calcium 24mg; Fibre 1.7g; Sodium 268mg.

Soy braised chicken

This is a classic Cantonese restaurant dish and is ideal to serve when entertaining, as it can be cooked up to a day in advance and simply reheated. Serve it with a sharp chilli, garlic and vinegar dip and plenty of sliced cucumber and rice.

SERVES 6–8

1 whole chicken (about 1.3kg/3lb)
25g/1oz/2 tbsp sugar
90ml/6 tbsp dark soy sauce
25g/1oz galangal, bruised
1.5 litres/2½ pints/6¼ cups water

10ml/2 tsp salt
15ml/1 tbsp cornflour
  (cornstarch)
steamed rice and sliced cucumber,
  to serve

1 Remove any excess fat from the chicken, wash it and pat dry. In a dry, heavy pan, heat the sugar until frothy and caramelized to a rich, dark brown colour. Add the chicken and turn it several times in the pan until well sealed.

2 Add the soy sauce, galangal and water. Bring to the boil and simmer, covered, for 30 minutes, turning several times so the chicken is evenly cooked.

3 Add the salt and continue to cook for another 15–20 minutes until tender. Remove and set aside.

4 Increase the heat and boil until the sauce is well reduced and glossy. Blend the cornflour with a little water, add to the sauce and cook, stirring until thickened.

5 Chop the chicken into bitesize pieces and serve with rice and sliced cucumber, with the sauce on the side.

Nutritional information per portion: Energy 255kcal/1058kJ; Protein 20.2g; Carbohydrate 5.9g, of which sugars 4.1g; Fat 16.8g, of which saturates 4.9g; Cholesterol 104mg; Calcium 12mg; Fibre 0g; Sodium 883mg.

Sichuan chicken with kung po sauce

*This recipe comes from the Sichuan region of Western China, where chillies are widely used.
Cashew nuts have become a popular ingredient in Chinese cooking.*

SERVES 3

**2 skinless, boneless chicken breast portions,
    total weight about 350g/12oz**
1 egg white
10ml/2 tsp cornflour (cornstarch)
2.5ml/¹/₂ tsp salt
30ml/2 tbsp yellow salted beans
15ml/1 tbsp hoisin sauce
5ml/1 tsp soft light brown sugar
15ml/1 tbsp rice wine or sherry
15ml/1 tbsp wine vinegar
4 garlic cloves, crushed
150ml/¹/₄ pint/²/₃ cup chicken stock
45ml/3 tbsp sunflower oil
2–3 dried red chillies, chopped
115g/4oz/1 cup roasted cashew nuts
fresh coriander (cilantro), to garnish

1 Cut the chicken into neat pieces. Lightly whisk the egg white in a dish,
whisk in the cornflour and salt, then add the chicken and stir until coated.

2 In a bowl, mash the beans. Stir in the hoisin sauce, brown sugar, rice wine
or sherry, vinegar, garlic and stock.

3 Heat a wok, add the oil and stir-fry the chicken for 2 minutes until tender.
Lift out the chicken and set aside.

4 Heat the oil remaining in the wok and fry the chilli pieces for 1 minute.
Return the chicken to the wok and pour in the bean sauce mixture. Bring to
the boil, stir in the cashew nuts and heat through. Spoon into a heated
serving dish, garnish with the coriander and serve immediately.

Nutritional information per portion: Energy 490kcal/2040kJ; Protein 37.7g; Carbohydrate 12.4g, of which sugars 2.6g;
Fat 31.9g, of which saturates 5.6g; Cholesterol 82mg; Calcium 24mg; Fibre 1.9g; Sodium 204mg.

Salt "baked" chicken

This is a wonderful way of cooking chicken. All the delicious, succulent juices are sealed firmly inside the salty crust – yet the flavour of the chicken isn't salty.

SERVES 8

1.5 kg/3–3½lb corn fed chicken
1.5 ml/¼ tsp salt
2.25kg/5lb coarse rock salt
15ml/1 tbsp vegetable oil
2.5cm/1 in piece fresh root ginger, finely chopped
4 spring onions (scallions), cut into fine rings
boiled rice, garnished with shredded spring onions, to serve

COOK'S TIP

The dry salt around the top of the chicken can be used again, but the salt from under the bird should be thrown away, as this will have absorbed fat and cooking juices.

1 Rinse the chicken, dry with kitchen paper and rub the inside with the fine salt. Place four pieces of damp kitchen paper on the bottom of a wok just large enough to hold the chicken. Sprinkle a layer of rock salt over the kitchen paper, about 1cm/½in thick. Place the chicken on top of the salt.

2 Pour the remaining salt over the chicken until it is completely covered. Dampen six more pieces of kitchen paper and place these around the rim of the wok. Cover and put the wok over a high heat for 10 minutes.

3 Reduce the heat to medium and continue to cook the chicken for 30 minutes without lifting the lid. Turn off the heat and leave for 10 minutes before lifting the chicken out of the salt. Brush off any salt that clings to the chicken and allow to cool for 20 minutes before cutting it into serving-size pieces.

4 Heat the oil in a frying pan until very hot. Add the ginger and spring onions and fry for a few seconds, then pour into a bowl and use as a dipping sauce for the chicken. Serve with boiled rice, garnished with shredded spring onions.

Nutritional information per portion: Energy 259kcal/1076kJ; Protein 23.4g; Carbohydrate 0.2g, of which sugars 0.1g; Fat 18.3g, of which saturates 4.9g; Cholesterol 124mg; Calcium 10mg; Fibre 0.1g; Sodium 2295mg.

Chicken with mixed vegetables

Chinese cooks are experts in making delicious dishes from a relatively small amount of meat and a lot of vegetables. Good news for anyone trying to eat less fat.

SERVES 4

350g/12oz skinless chicken breast fillets
20ml/4 tsp vegetable oil
300ml/1/2 pint/11/4 cups chicken stock
75g/3oz/3/4 cup drained, canned straw
   mushrooms
50g/2oz/1/2 cup sliced, drained, canned
   bamboo shoots
50g/2oz/1/3 cup drained, canned water
   chestnuts, sliced
1 small carrot, sliced
50g/2oz/1/2 cup mangetouts (snow peas)
15ml/1 tbsp dry sherry
15ml/1 tbsp oyster sauce
5ml/1 tsp caster (superfine) sugar
5ml/1 tsp cornflour (cornstarch)
15ml/1 tbsp cold water
salt and ground white pepper

1 Put the chicken in a shallow bowl. Add 5ml/1 tsp of the oil, 1.5ml/1/4 tsp salt and a pinch of pepper. Cover and set aside for 10 minutes in a cool place.

2 Bring the stock to the boil in a pan. Add the chicken fillets and cook for 12 minutes, or until tender.

3 Drain and slice the chicken, reserving 75ml/5 tbsp of the stock.

4 Heat the remaining oil in a wok, add all the vegetables and stir-fry for 2 minutes. Stir in the sherry, oyster sauce, caster sugar and reserved stock. Add the chicken to the pan and cook for 2 minutes more.

5 Mix the cornflour to a paste with the water. Add the mixture to the pan and cook, stirring, until thickened. Season to taste with salt and pepper and serve immediately.

Nutritional information per portion: Energy 154kcal/646kJ; Protein 22.2g; Carbohydrate 4.9g, of which sugars 3.4g; Fat 4.3g, of which saturates 0.7g; Cholesterol 61mg; Calcium 17mg; Fibre 1g; Sodium 61mg.

Chicken with young ginger

Ginger plays a big role in Chinese cooking, particularly in stir-fried dishes. Whenever possible, juicy and pungent young ginger is used. This is a simple and delicious way to cook chicken, pork or beef.

SERVES 4

30ml/2 tbsp groundnut (peanut) oil
3 garlic cloves, finely sliced in strips
50g/2oz fresh young root ginger, finely
**   sliced in strips**
2 fresh red chillies, seeded and finely
**   sliced in strips**
4 chicken breast fillets or 4 boned
**   chicken legs, skinned and cut into**
**   bitesize chunks**
30ml/2 tbsp fish sauce
10ml/2 tsp sugar
a small bunch of coriander (cilantro),
**   stalks removed, roughly chopped**
ground black pepper
jasmine rice and crunchy salad, to serve

1 Heat a wok and add the oil. Add the garlic, ginger and chillies, and stir-fry until golden. Add the chicken and toss it around the wok for 1–2 minutes.

2 Stir in the fish sauce and sugar, and stir-fry for a further 4–5 minutes until cooked.

3 Season the chicken with black pepper and add some of the chopped fresh coriander.

4 Transfer the chicken to a serving dish and garnish with the remaining coriander. Serve hot with jasmine rice and a crunchy salad with fresh herbs, or with chunks of baguette

Nutritional information per portion: Energy 222kcal/935kJ; Protein 36.4g; Carbohydrate 3g, of which sugars 2.9g; Fat 7.3g, of which saturates 1.1g; Cholesterol 105mg; Calcium 32mg; Fibre 0.6g; Sodium 101mg.

Lemon and sesame chicken

These delicate strips of chicken are at their best if you have time to leave them to marinate overnight so that they can really soak up the flavours. The subtle fragrance of lemon really enhances the rich taste of fried chicken and the nutty sesame seeds.

SERVES 4

4 large chicken breast fillets,
    skinned and cut into strips
15ml/1 tbsp light soy sauce
15ml/1 tbsp rice wine
2 garlic cloves, crushed
10ml/2 tsp finely grated fresh
    root ginger
1 egg, lightly beaten
150g/5oz cornflour (cornstarch)
sunflower oil, for deep-frying
toasted sesame seeds, to sprinkle
rice or noodles, to serve

FOR THE SAUCE
15ml/1 tbsp sunflower oil
2 spring onions (scallions),
    finely sliced
1 garlic clove, crushed
10ml/2 tsp cornflour (cornstarch)
90ml/6 tbsp chicken stock
10ml/2 tsp finely grated lemon rind
30ml/2 tbsp fresh lemon juice
10ml/2 tsp sugar
2.5ml/1/2 tsp sesame oil
salt

1 Place the chicken strips in a large, non-metallic bowl. Mix together the light soy sauce, rice wine, garlic and ginger and pour over the chicken. Toss together to combine.

2 Cover the chicken and place in the refrigerator for 8–10 hours, or overnight if time permits.

3 When ready to cook, add the beaten egg to the chicken and mix well, then put the mixture into a colander to drain off any excess marinade and egg.

4 Place the cornflour in a large plastic bag and add the chicken pieces. Shake it vigorously to thoroughly coat the chicken strips.

5 Fill a wok one-third full of sunflower oil and heat to 180°C/350°F (or until a cube of bread, dropped into the oil, browns in 15 seconds).

6 Deep-fry the chicken, in batches, for 3–4 minutes. Lift out the chicken using a slotted spoon and drain on kitchen paper. Reheat the oil and deep-fry the chicken once more, in batches, for 2–3 minutes. Remove with a slotted spoon and drain on kitchen paper. Pour the oil out and wipe out the wok with kitchen paper.

7 To make the sauce, heat the sunflower oil in a wok. Add the spring onions and garlic and stir-fry for 1–2 minutes. Mix together the cornflour, stock, lemon rind, lemon juice, sugar, sesame oil and salt and pour into the wok. Cook over a high heat for 2–3 minutes until thickened. Return the chicken to the sauce, toss lightly and sprinkle over the toasted sesame seeds. Serve with rice or noodles.

Nutritional information per portion: Energy 450kcal/1891kJ; Protein 38.2g; Carbohydrate 37.1g, of which sugars 2.5g; Fat 17.6g, of which saturates 2.6g; Cholesterol 157mg; Calcium 25mg; Fibre 0.1g; Sodium 396mg.

Lemon chicken

This is a perfect balance of flavours between the richness of the fried chicken and the sweet-sour lemon sauce. The egg and cornflour coating has a wonderfully crisp texture.

SERVES 4

2 chicken breasts, skinned
1 egg, lightly beaten
30ml/2 tbsp cornflour (cornstarch)
vegetable or groundnut (peanut) oil,
    for deep-frying
salt

FOR THE SAUCE
45ml/3 tbsp lemon juice
5ml/1 tsp ground turmeric
15ml/1 tbsp sugar or to taste
15ml/1 tbsp plum sauce
175ml/6fl oz water
5ml/1 tbsp cornflour (cornstarch)

1 Slice each chicken breast across the thickest part to give two thin escalopes. Dip the chicken breasts lightly in beaten egg and coat with cornflour. Heat the oil in a wok or large pan and deep-fry the chicken until golden brown. Keep warm.

2 Mix together all the sauce ingredients, except the cornflour, stirring well to avoid lumps. Bring the sauce to a slow simmer in a small pan and cook for 2 minutes. Blend the cornflour with a little water and add, a little at a time, until the sauce is the consistency of thin cream. Season to taste with salt.

3 Slice the chicken into 2.5cm/1in strips and place on a serving plate. Pour the sauce over and serve garnished with lemon wedges.

Nutritional information per portion: Energy 231kcal/975kJ; Protein 30.1g; Carbohydrate 13.1g, of which sugars 13.1g; Fat 6.9g, of which saturates 1.2g; Cholesterol 88mg; Calcium 13mg; Fibre 0g; Sodium 76mg.

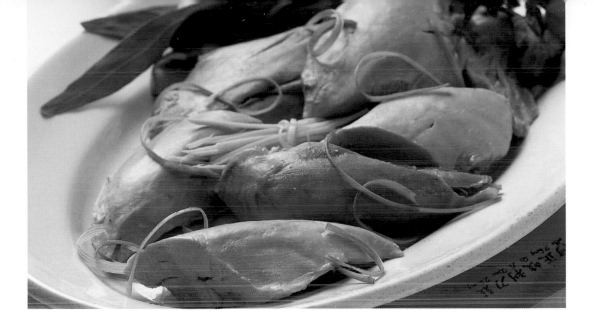

Drunken chicken

In this traditional dish, cooked chicken is marinated in sherry, fresh root ginger and spring onions for several days. Because of the lengthy preparation time, it is important to use a very fresh bird.

SERVES 4–6

1 chicken, about 1.3kg/3lb
1cm/¹⁄₂in piece of fresh root ginger, thinly sliced
2 spring onions (scallions), trimmed, plus extra to garnish
300ml/¹⁄₂ pint/1¹⁄₄ cups dry sherry
salt

1 Rinse and dry the chicken. Place the ginger and spring onions in the body cavity. Put the chicken in a large pan and just cover with water. Bring to the boil, skim off any scum and cook for 15 minutes.

2 Remove from the heat, cover the pan tightly and leave the chicken in the cooking liquid for 3–4 hours, until cooked. Drain, reserving the stock. Pour 300ml/¹⁄₂ pint/1¹⁄₄ cups of the stock into a jug (pitcher).

3 Remove the skin and neatly portion the chicken. Arrange the chicken in a shallow dish. Rub salt into the chicken and cover with clear film (plastic wrap). Leave in a cool place for several hours or overnight in the refrigerator.

4 Lift off any fat from the measured stock, add the sherry and pour over the chicken. Cover again and leave in the refrigerator to marinate for 2–3 days, turning occasionally. When ready to serve, cut the chicken into chunky pieces and arrange on a serving platter. Garnish with spring onion shreds.

VARIATION
To serve as a cocktail snack, take the meat off the bones, cut it into bitesize pieces, then spear each piece on a cocktail stick (toothpick).

Nutritional information per portion: Energy 608kcal/2553kJ; Protein 35.4g; Carbohydrate 52.7g, of which sugars 29g; Fat 17.6g, of which saturates 1.9g; Cholesterol 82mg; Calcium 107mg; Fibre 3.7g; Sodium 97mg.

Peking duck with Mandarin pancakes

As the Chinese discovered centuries ago, this is quite the best way to eat duck. The preparation is time-consuming, but it can be done in easy stages and is well worth the effort.

SERVES 6

1 duck, about 2.25kg/5¼lb
45ml/3 tbsp clear honey
30ml/2 tbsp water
5ml/1 tsp salt
a bunch spring onions (scallions),
    cut into strips
½ cucumber, seeded and
    cut into matchsticks

FOR THE MANDARIN PANCAKES

275g/10oz/2½ cups strong white bread flour
5ml/1 tsp salt
45ml/3 tbsp groundnut (peanut) or sesame oil
250ml/8fl oz/1 cup boiling water

FOR THE DIPPING SAUCES

120ml/4fl oz/½ cup hoisin sauce
120ml/4fl oz/½ cup plum sauce

1 Bring a large pan of water to the boil. Place the duck on a trivet in the sink and pour the boiling water over the duck to scald. Carefully lift it out on the trivet and drain thoroughly. Tie string firmly around its legs and suspend it in a cool room. Place a bowl underneath to catch the drips and leave overnight.

2 Next day, blend the honey, water and salt and brush half the mixture over the duck skin. Hang up again and leave for 2–3 hours. Repeat and leave to dry completely for a further 3–4 hours.

3 Make the pancakes. Sift the flour and salt into a bowl or food processor. Add 15ml/1 tbsp of the oil, then gradually add enough of the boiling water to form a soft but not sticky dough. Knead for 2–3 minutes by hand or for 30 seconds in the food processor. Allow to rest for 30 minutes. Knead the dough again, then divide it into 24 pieces and roll each piece to a 15cm/6in round. Brush the surface of half the rounds with oil, then sandwich the rounds together in pairs.

4 Brush the surface of two heavy frying pans sparingly with oil. Add one pancake pair to each pan and cook for 2–3 minutes until cooked but not coloured. Turn over and cook for 2–3 minutes more. Slide the double pancakes out of the pan and pull them apart. Stack on a plate, placing a square of baking parchment between each while cooking the remainder. Cool, wrap tightly in foil and set aside.

5 Preheat the oven to 230°C/450°F/Gas 8. When it reaches that temperature, put the duck on a rack in a roasting pan and place it in the oven. Immediately reduce the temperature to 180°C/350°F/Gas 4 and roast the duck for 1¾ hours without basting. Check that the skin is crisp and, if it is not, increase the oven temperature to the maximum. Roast for 15 minutes more.

6 Meanwhile, place the spring onion strips in iced water to crisp up. Drain. Pat the cucumber pieces dry on kitchen paper. Reheat the prepared pancakes by steaming the foil parcel for 5–10 minutes in a bamboo steamer over a wok or pan of boiling water. Pour the dipping sauces into small dishes to share between the guests.

7 Carve the duck into 4cm/1½in pieces. At the table, each guest smears some of the prepared sauce on a pancake, tops it with a small amount of crisp duck skin and meat and adds cucumber and spring onion strips before enjoying the rolled-up pancake.

Nutritional information per portion: Energy 174kcal/734kJ; Protein 16.9g; Carbohydrate 14.9g, of which sugars 4.7g; Fat 5.3g, of which saturates 1.7g; Cholesterol 85mg; Calcium 21mg; Fibre 0.7g; Sodium 334mg.

Chinese duck curry

This richly spiced curry illustrates how five-spice powder marries the flavours of duck, ginger and butternut squash. The duck tastes good even if you only have time to marinate it briefly.

SERVES 4

4 duck breast portions, skinned
30ml/2 tbsp five-spice powder
30ml/2 tbsp sesame oil
grated rind and juice of 1 orange
1 medium butternut squash,
    peeled and cubed
10ml/2 tsp red curry paste
30ml/2 tbsp fish sauce
15ml/1 tbsp palm sugar (jaggery) or
    light muscovado (brown) sugar
300ml/½ pint/1¼ cups coconut milk
2 fresh red chillies, seeded
4 kaffir lime leaves, torn
a small bunch of coriander (cilantro),
    chopped, to garnish
noodles, to serve

1 Cut the duck meat into bitesize pieces and put in a bowl with the five-spice powder, sesame oil and orange rind and juice. Stir well to coat the duck in the marinade. Cover the bowl with clear film (plastic wrap) and set aside in a cool place to marinate for at least 15 minutes.

2 Bring a pan of water to the boil. Add the squash and cook for 10–15 minutes, until just tender. Drain well and set aside.

3 Pour the marinade from the duck into a wok and heat until boiling. Stir in the curry paste and cook for 2–3 minutes, until fragrant. Add the duck and cook for 3–4 minutes, stirring, until browned on all sides.

4 Add the fish sauce and sugar and cook for 2 minutes more. Stir in the coconut milk, then add the cooked squash, with the chillies and lime leaves. Simmer gently for 5 minutes, then spoon into a dish, sprinkle with the coriander and serve with noodles.

Nutritional information per portion: Energy 295kcal/1241kJ; Protein 31.4g; Carbohydrate 13.3g, of which sugars 12.3g; Fat 15.9g, of which saturates 3.1g; Cholesterol 165mg; Calcium 102mg; Fibre 2g; Sodium 427mg.

Braised duck in aromatic sauce

The Chinese often braise meat in soy sauce and warm flavourings, such as star anise and cinnamon. Chillies are always tucked into the recipe to achieve a desirable fiery kick.

SERVES 4–6

1 duck (about 2kg/4¹/₂ lb), washed
15–30ml/1–2 tbsp five-spice powder
25g/1oz fresh turmeric, chopped
25g/1oz galangal, chopped
4 garlic cloves, chopped
30ml/2 tbsp sesame oil
12 shallots, peeled and left whole
2–3 lemon grass stalks, lightly crushed
4 cinnamon sticks
8 star anise
12 cloves
600ml/1 pint/2¹/₂ cups light soy sauce
120ml/4fl oz/¹/₂ cup dark soy sauce
30–45ml/2–3 tbsp palm sugar (jaggery)
coriander (cilantro) leaves, to garnish
4 chillies, seeded and quartered, to garnish
steamed jasmine rice and salad, to serve

1 Rub the duck, inside and out, with the five-spice powder and place in the refrigerator for 6–8 hours, uncovered.

2 Using a mortar and pestle, grind the turmeric, galangal and garlic to a smooth paste.

3 Heat the oil in a heavy pan and stir in the spice paste until it becomes fragrant.

4 Stir in the shallots, lemon grass, cinnamon sticks, star anise and cloves. Pour in the soy sauces and stir in the sugar until dissolved.

5 Place the duck in the pan, baste with the sauce, and add 550ml/18fl oz/2¹/₂ cups water. Bring to the boil, reduce the heat and cover the pan. Simmer for 4–6 hours, until the duck is very tender. Garnish with coriander and chillies, and serve with rice.

Nutritional information per portion: Energy 119kcal/498kJ; Protein 10.2g; Carbohydrate 4.6g, of which sugars 3.4g; Fat 6.9g, of which saturates 1.5g; Cholesterol 50mg; Calcium 35mg; Fibre 1.1g; Sodium 412mg.

Duck and sesame stir-fry

This recipe is intended for game birds, and also works well with pheasant or partridge. If you use farmed duck, you should remove the skin and fat layer as it is fattier than wild duck.

SERVES 4

250g/9oz skinless wild duck
    breast fillets
15ml/1 tbsp sesame oil
15ml/1 tbsp vegetable oil
4 garlic cloves, finely sliced
2.5ml/¹/₂ tsp dried chilli flakes
15ml/1 tbsp fish sauce
15ml/1 tbsp light soy sauce
120ml/4fl oz/¹/₂ cup water
1 head broccoli, cut into small florets
coriander (cilantro) and 15ml/1 tbsp
    toasted sesame seeds, to garnish

1 Cut the duck into bitesize pieces. Heat the oils in a wok or large frying pan and stir-fry the garlic over a medium heat until it is golden brown – do not let it burn.

2 Add the duck pieces to the pan and stir-fry for a further 2 minutes, until the meat begins to brown.

3 Stir in the chilli flakes, fish sauce, soy sauce and water. Add the broccoli florets and continue to stir-fry the mixture for about 2 minutes, until the duck pieces are just cooked through.

4 Serve immediately on warmed plates, garnished with sprigs of coriander and sesame seeds.

Nutritional information per portion: Energy 156kcal/651kJ; Protein 16.3g; Carbohydrate 1.9g, of which sugars 1.6g; Fat 10.4g, of which saturates 1.7g; Cholesterol 69mg; Calcium 58mg; Fibre 2.3g; Sodium 343mg.

Cantonese roast duck

Possibly one of the best-known duck dishes around the world, this should have really crackly, crisp skin. The traditional method used in China is to dry the duck in the sun for at least six hours.

SERVES 6-8

1 prepared duck (about 1.5kg/3¹/₂lb),
    trimmed of excess fat
30ml/2 tbsp hoisin sauce
30ml/2 tbsp rice wine or sherry
1 small cube preserved red soy bean,
    finely mashed
a few drops cochineal, or red food
    colouring
chilli sauce, to serve

1 Tie a length of string under the wings and around the neck of the duck to make a loop. Bring a pot of water to the boil and use the string to immerse the duck several times.

2 Hang up the duck for several hours, or overnight. The skin will take on a parchment-like texture as it dries out.

3 Preheat the oven to 220°C/425°F/Gas 7. Blend the hoisin sauce, rice wine, red soy bean and red colouring and rub all over the duck.

4 Place the duck on a rack in a roasting pan and roast for 30 minutes. Reduce the heat to 180°C/350°F/Gas 4 and cook for another 30 minutes. Push a metal skewer between the thigh and breast – if the juice runs clear the duck is done.

5 Turn off the heat and leave the duck in the oven for 20 minutes to continue cooking.

6 Chop the duck into portions and serve with a chilli sauce dip.

Nutritional information per portion: Energy 384kcal/1581kJ; Protein 10g; Carbohydrate 0.7g, of which sugars 0.7g; Fat 37.4g, of which saturates 10.2g; Cholesterol 0mg; Calcium 11mg; Fibre 0g; Sodium 232mg.

Meat

Pork and beef are the most widely-used meats in Chinese cuisine, although lamb and mutton are occasionally used. This chapter includes sumptuous meat dishes for every occasion, from midweek meals to elegant dishes for entertaining. Included are gloriously sticky Pork Ribs in Black Bean Sauce, a piquant Mongolian Firepot and quick and healthy Sichuan Beef with Tofu.

Pork ribs in black bean sauce

Black beans and black bean sauce go particularly well with pork. Boiling the ribs first ensures a more succulent texture and the meat absorbs the seasonings better.

SERVES 4

8 large meaty pork spare ribs
500ml/17fl oz/generous 2 cups water
30ml/2 tbsp light soy sauce
15g/¹/₂oz fresh root ginger
3 garlic cloves
2 red chillies
45ml/3 tbsp sesame oil
30ml/2 tbsp black bean sauce

1 Cut each rib into 6cm/2¹/₂in pieces. Bring the water to the boil in a wok or heavy pan and add the soy sauce. Add the ribs and cook for 20 minutes. Drain, reserving the stock for another dish.

2 Finely chop the ginger, garlic and chillies. Blend the sesame oil with the black bean sauce and add the ginger, garlic and chillies.

3 Pour the mixture over the cooked ribs in a shallow dish and leave to marinate for several hours.

4 When ready to cook, lift the ribs out of the marinade and arrange them in a shallow dish. Put the dish in a bamboo steamer, cover and steam the ribs for about 15 minutes until they are heated through and tender.

Nutritional information per portion: Energy 722kcal/3012kJ; Protein 61.8g; Carbohydrate 2.6g, of which sugars 1g; Fat 51.9g, of which saturates 18.1g; Cholesterol 215mg; Calcium 59mg; Fibre 0.7g; Sodium 897mg.

Chinese braised pork belly with Asian greens

Pork belly becomes meltingly tender in this slow-braised dish flavoured with orange, cinnamon, star anise and ginger. The flavours meld and mellow during cooking to produce a rich, complex taste.

SERVES 4

800g/1³/₄lb pork belly, trimmed
    and cut into 12 pieces
400ml/14fl oz/1²/₃ cups beef stock
75ml/5 tbsp soy sauce
finely grated rind and juice
    of 1 large orange
15ml/1 tbsp finely shredded fresh
    root ginger
2 garlic cloves, sliced
15ml/1 tbsp hot chilli powder
15ml/1 tbsp dark muscovado (molasses)
    sugar
3 cinnamon sticks
3 cloves
10 black peppercorns
2–3 star anise
steamed greens and rice, to serve

1 Place the pork in a wok and pour over water to cover. Bring the water to the boil. Cover, reduce the heat and cook gently for 30 minutes. Drain the pork and return to the wok with the stock, soy sauce, orange rind and juice, ginger, garlic, chilli powder, muscovado sugar, cinnamon sticks, cloves, peppercorns and star anise.

2 Pour over water to just cover the pork belly pieces and cook on a high heat until it comes to the boil.

3 Cover the wok tightly with a lid, then reduce the heat to low and cook gently for 1½ hours, stirring occasionally. (Check the pork occasionally during cooking to ensure it doesn't stick to the base of the wok.)

4 Uncover the wok and simmer for 30 minutes, stirring occasionally until the meat is very tender. Serve immediately with steamed greens and rice.

Nutritional information per portion: Energy 543kcal/2260kJ; Protein 38.9g; Carbohydrate 6.6g, of which sugars 6.4g; Fat 40.4g, of which saturates 14.6g; Cholesterol 142mg; Calcium 19mg; Fibre 0g; Sodium 1475mg

Cantonese roast pork

This classic is based on a pork rib cut that is a mixture of fat and lean meat. Traditionally, chefs use a special clay oven. However, a convection oven will work if you use a rack set in a roasting pan.

SERVES 8

900g/2lb pork rib-eye steak, in one piece
30ml/2 tbsp honey
30ml/2 tbsp hoisin sauce
15ml/1 tbsp preserved red bean curd
30ml/2 tbsp rice wine
sliced cucumber and a hot chilli sauce dip,
   to serve

1 If the piece of steak is 7.5cm/3in thick or more, cut it in half horizontally. Score the surface at regular intervals to a depth of about 1cm/½in.

2 In a dish that is large enough to allow the piece or pieces of meat to lie flat, mix the honey with the hoisin sauce. Add the preserved red bean curd, mashing it so that it combines with the other ingredients. Stir in the wine.

3 Add the pork and rub it all over with the marinade, making sure to penetrate the scored cuts. Cover the dish and marinate the pork for 1 hour or overnight.

4 Preheat the oven to 220°C/425°F/Gas 7. Place the pork on a rack set in a roasting pan. Roast the pork for 20 minutes, then reduce the oven temperature to 180°C/350°F/Gas 4 and roast for 20 minutes more.

5 Preheat the grill (broiler). Place the pork under the heat until the surface chars lightly in places. Let the pork cool. Serve sliced, with cucumber and chilli sauce.

Nutritional information per portion: Energy 158kcal/664kJ; Protein 24.3g; Carbohydrate 4g, of which sugars 4g; Fat 4.6g, of which saturates 1.6g; Cholesterol 71mg; Calcium 18mg; Fibre 0g; Sodium 141mg.

Char-siu pork

Marinated pork fillet, roasted and glazed with honey and spices, is irresistible on its own and can also be used as the basis for delicious salads and stir-fries.

SERVES 6

15ml/1 tbsp vegetable oil
15ml/1 tbsp hoisin sauce
15ml/1 tbsp yellow bean sauce
1.5ml/¼ tsp five spice powder
2.5ml/½ tsp cornflour (cornstarch)
15ml/1 tbsp caster (superfine) sugar
1.5ml/¼ tsp salt
1.5ml/¼ tsp ground white pepper
450g/1 lb pork fillet, trimmed
10ml/2 tsp clear honey
shredded spring onion (scallions),
    to garnish
rice, to serve

1 Mix the oil, sauces, five-spice powder, cornflour, sugar and seasoning in a shallow dish. Add the pork and coat it with the mixture. Cover and chill for 4 hours or overnight.

2 Preheat the oven to 190°C/375°F/Gas 5. Drain the pork and place it on a wire rack over a deep roasting pan. Roast for 40 minutes, turning the pork over from time to time.

3 Check that the pork is cooked by inserting a skewer or fork into the meat; the juices should run clear. If they are still tinged with pink, roast the pork for 5–10 minutes more.

4 Remove the pork from the oven and brush it with the honey. Allow to cool for 10 minutes before cutting into slices. Garnish with spring onions and serve hot or cold with rice.

Nutritional information per portion: Energy 135kcal/568kJ; Protein 16.2g; Carbohydrate 7.1g, of which sugars 6.6g; Fat 4.9g, of which saturates 1.3g; Cholesterol 47mg; Calcium 8mg; Fibre 0.1g; Sodium 175mg.

Sweet and sour pork

This classic Chinese dish with its stunning colours and sweet, sour, piquant sauce and gloriously sticky texture is always popular. Serve it with egg fried rice and steamed Asian greens to create an authentic and truly rewarding Chinese meal.

SERVES 4

45ml/3 tbsp light soy sauce

15ml/1 tbsp rice wine

15ml/1 tbsp sesame oil

5ml/1 tsp ground black pepper

500g/1¼lb pork loin, cut into
   1cm/½in cubes

65g/2½oz/9 tbsp cornflour (cornstarch)

65g/2½oz/9 tbsp plain (all-purpose) flour

5ml/1 tsp bicarbonate of soda (baking soda)

sunflower oil, for deep-frying

10ml/2 tsp finely grated garlic

5ml/1 tsp finely grated fresh root ginger

60ml/4 tbsp tomato ketchup

30ml/2 tbsp caster (superfine) sugar

15ml/1 tbsp rice vinegar

15ml/1 tbsp cornflour (cornstarch)
   blended with 120ml/4fl oz/½ cup water

4 spring onions (scallions), shredded

1 carrot, shredded

1 red (bell) pepper, shredded

egg fried rice, to serve

salt

1 In a large bowl, combine 15ml/1 tbsp of the soy sauce with the rice wine, sesame oil and pepper. Add the pork and mix. Cover and chill for 3–4 hours.

2 Combine the cornflour, plain flour and bicarbonate of soda in a bowl. Add a pinch of salt and mix in 150ml/¼ pint/⅔ cup cold water to make a batter. Add the pork to the batter and mix well with your hands to coat.

3 Fill a wok one-third full with the sunflower oil and heat to 180°C/350°F (or until a cube of bread browns in 45 seconds). Separate the pork cubes and deep-fry them, in batches, for 1–2 minutes, or until golden. Remove and drain on kitchen paper.

4 Place a clean wok over a medium heat. Mix together the garlic, ginger, tomato ketchup, sugar, the remaining soy sauce, rice vinegar and cornflour mixture. Add to the wok and stir for 2–3 minutes, until thickened. Add the spring onions, carrot and red pepper, stir and remove from the heat.

5 Reheat the deep-frying oil in the wok to 180°C/350°F and then re-fry the pork in batches for 1–2 minutes, until golden and crisp. Drain, add to the sauce and toss to mix well. Serve with egg fried rice.

Nutritional information per portion: Energy 727kcal/3035kJ; Protein 32.8g; Carbohydrate 76.5g, of which sugars 39.4g; Fat 32.8g, of which saturates 5.8g; Cholesterol 272mg; Calcium 85mg; Fibre 2.7g; Sodium 1048mg.

Pork in preserved tofu

Cantonese chefs use two main types of preserved tofu: this recipe uses a red one, known as lam yee. It has an intense flavour, and also gives the dish a very attractive bright red colour.

SERVES 4

450g/1lb pork rib-eye steak streaked
   with a little fat
15ml/1 tbsp cornflour (cornstarch)
1/2 large onion
2 garlic cloves
30ml/2 tbsp vegetable oil
30ml/2 tbsp preserved red tofu
5ml/1 tsp sugar
120ml/4fl oz/1/2 cup water
rice or noodles, to serve

1 With a sharp knife, cut the pork into thin slices. Put the cornflour in a bowl or strong plastic bag, add the pork and toss lightly to coat.

2 Slice the onion and garlic finely. Heat the oil in a wok and fry the onion for 2 minutes. Add the garlic and fry for 1 minute. Push the onion and garlic to the sides of the wok and add the pork slices to the centre. Stir-fry for 2–3 minutes, until the pork is sealed. Mix the pork with the onion mixture.

3 Add the red tofu and mash with a ladle or a fork. Continue to stir-fry the mixture until the pork is thoroughly coated in the tofu.

4 Add the sugar and water and bring to the boil. When the sauce has reduced to half the volume, the pork should be done. Serve hot with rice or noodles.

Nutritional information per portion: Energy 215kcal/898kJ; Protein 24.9g; Carbohydrate 5.7g, of which sugars 1.9g; Fat 10.4g, of which saturates 2.3g; Cholesterol 71mg; Calcium 51mg; Fibre 0.2g; Sodium 82mg.

Stewed mutton with tofu sticks

Dry tofu sticks, called fu choke in Cantonese, are pale yellow in colour. They have rather a bland taste, but are the perfect foil for rich meats like mutton and lamb.

SERVES 4

350g/12oz lean mutton or lamb
15ml/1 tbsp vegetable oil
3 garlic cloves, sliced
5ml/1 tsp sugar
45ml/3 tbsp dark soy sauce
pinch of five-spice powder
600ml/1 pint/2½ cups water
2.5ml/½ tsp ground black pepper
100g/3¼oz tofu sticks, soaked in hot
   water for 30 minutes, until soft

1 Cut the meat into bitesize chunks and tenderize using a meat mallet.

2 Heat the oil in a wok and fry the garlic until golden brown. Add the meat and fry for 2 minutes to seal in the flavour. Sprinkle the sugar over the meat, then stir in the soy sauce, five-spice powder, water and pepper. Transfer the mixture to a pan, cover with a lid and cook over medium heat for 30 minutes.

3 Cut the tofu sticks into 5cm/2in lengths. Stir them into the stew, then replace the lid and simmer for 20 minutes more.

4 Remove the lid, increase the heat to high and cook for a further 10 minutes to reduce the sauce. Spoon the stew into a heated dish and serve immediately.

Nutritional information per portion: Energy 209kcal/870kJ; Protein 19.5g; Carbohydrate 2.2g, of which sugars 2g; Fat 13.6g, of which saturates 5g; Cholesterol 67mg; Calcium 137mg; Fibre 0g; Sodium 877mg.

Mongolian firepot

This mode of cooking was introduced to China by the Mongols in the 13th century. Guests cook the ingredients at the table, dipping the meats in a variety of sauces, then a soup is made with the stock and Chinese leaves, spinach, tofu and noodles.

SERVES 6–8

900g/2lb boned leg of lamb, preferably bought
    thinly sliced
225g/8oz lamb's liver and/or kidneys
900ml/1½ pints/3¾ cups lamb stock
900ml/1½ pints/3¾ cups chicken stock
1cm/½in piece fresh root ginger, thinly sliced
45ml/3 tbsp rice wine or medium dry sherry
½ head Chinese leaves (Chinese cabbage),
    shredded
a few young spinach leaves
250g/9oz firm tofu, diced
115g/4oz cellophane noodles
salt and ground black pepper

FOR THE DIPPING SAUCE

50ml/2fl oz/¼ cup red wine vinegar
7.5ml/½ tbsp dark soy sauce
1cm/½in piece fresh root ginger,
    finely shredded
1 spring onion (scallion),
    finely shredded

TO SERVE

crusty bread
bowls of tomato ketchup, sweet chilli sauce,
    mustard oil and sesame oil
dry-fried coriander seeds, crushed

1 Ask your butcher to slice the lamb thinly on a slicing machine, if possible. If you have had to buy it in a piece, however, put it in the freezer for about an hour, so that it is easier to slice thinly.

2 Trim the liver and remove the skin and core from the kidneys, if using. Place them in the freezer too. If you managed to buy sliced lamb, keep it in the refrigerator until needed.

3 Mix both types of stock in a large pan. Add the sliced ginger and rice wine or sherry and season with salt and pepper to taste. Heat to simmering point and simmer for 15 minutes.

4 Slice all the meats thinly and arrange them attractively on a large platter.

5 Place the Chinese leaves, spinach and tofu on a platter. Soak the noodles, following the instructions on the packet.

6 Make the dipping sauce by mixing all the ingredients in a small bowl. The other sauces and the crushed coriander seeds should be spooned into separate small dishes and placed on a serving tray.

7 Fill the moat of the hotpot with the simmering stock. Alternatively, fill a fondue pot and place it over a burner. Each guest selects a portion of meat from the platter and cooks it in the hot stock, using chopsticks or a fondue fork. The meat is then dipped in one of the sauces and coated with the coriander seeds (if liked) before being eaten with a chunk of crusty bread.

8 When all or most of the meat has been cooked and eaten, top up the stock, if necessary, then add the Chinese leaves, spinach leaves, tofu and drained noodles. Cook for 1–2 minutes, until the noodles are tender and the vegetables are cooked, but retain a little crispness. Ladle the soup into warmed bowls and serve with any remaining crusty bread.

Nutritional information per portion: Energy 144kcal/606kJ; Protein 12.3g; Carbohydrate 12g, of which sugars 1.2g; Fat 5.1g, of which saturates 1.1g; Cholesterol 128mg; Calcium 193mg; Fibre 0.9g; Sodium 49mg.

Sichuan beef with tofu

China's western province is famous for its spicy cuisine. Sichuan peppercorns, which feature in this dish, are the dried berries of a type of ash tree, and they do have a very peppery flavour.

SERVES 4

200g/7oz/1 cup Thai fragrant or
   basmati rice
30ml/2 tbsp groundnut (peanut)
   or soya oil
4 garlic cloves, finely chopped
600g/1lb 6oz beef steak, cut into
   thin strips
500g/1¼lb firm tofu, drained and diced
1 head broccoli, coarsely chopped
90ml/6 tbsp soy sauce
a pinch of sugar
juice of 1 lime
ground Sichuan peppercorns
sweet chilli sauce, to serve (optional)

1 Cook the rice in salted boiling water until tender, according to the instructions on the packet, then set aside.

2 Heat the oil in a large non-stick wok or frying pan, then add the garlic and stir-fry for a few seconds, until golden. Increase the heat to high, add the strips of steak and stir-fry briefly to seal.

3 Add the tofu cubes and chopped broccoli to the wok or frying pan and stir-fry for a few seconds. Stir in the soy sauce, sugar, lime juice and ground Sichuan peppercorns, then stir-fry for about 2 minutes.

4 Transfer the stir-fry to warm serving plates or bowls and serve immediately with the rice and chilli sauce, if you like.

Nutritional information per portion: Energy 646kcal/2694kJ; Protein 55g; Carbohydrate 46.9g, of which sugars 4.1g; Fat 26.2g, of which saturates 7.6g; Cholesterol 87mg; Calcium 731mg; Fibre 3.8g; Sodium 1714mg.

Stir-fried beef and mushrooms

The combination of garlic and salted black beans is a classic Cantonese seasoning that goes really well with the beef and mushrooms in this recipe. Serve with rice and simple braised Chinese greens.

SERVES 4

30ml/2 tbsp soy sauce
30ml/2 tbsp rice wine
10ml/2 tsp cornflour (cornstarch)
10ml/2 tsp sesame oil
450g/1lb fillet or rump (round) steak,
    trimmed of fat
12 dried Chinese mushrooms, soaked in
    boiling water for 25 minutes
25ml/1½ tbsp salted black beans
5ml/1 tsp caster (superfine) sugar
120ml/4fl oz/½ cup groundnut
    (peanut) oil
4 garlic cloves, thinly sliced
2.5cm/1in piece fresh root ginger, cut
    into fine strips
200g/7oz open cap
    mushrooms, sliced
1 bunch spring onions (scallions),
    sliced diagonally
1 fresh red chilli, seeded and
    finely shredded
salt and ground black pepper

1 In a bowl, mix half the soy sauce, half the rice wine, half the cornflour and all the sesame oil with 15ml/1 tbsp water until smooth. Season.

2 Thinly slice the beef. Add the slices to the cornflour mixture and rub into the beef. Set aside for 30 minutes.

3 Drain the mushrooms, reserving 45ml/3 tbsp of the water. Discard the stalks and cut the caps in half.

4 Mash the black beans with the caster sugar in a bowl. Stir the rest of the cornflour, soy sauce and rice wine together In another bowl.

5 Heat the oil in a wok, then fry the beef until brown. Transfer to a plate, leaving 45ml/3 tbsp of oil in the wok.

6 Add the garlic and ginger, stir-fry for 1 minute, then add all of the mushrooms and stir-fry for 2 minutes. Add the spring onions and black beans and fry for another 1–2 minutes.

7 Return the beef to the wok, then add 45ml/3 tbsp of the shiitake soaking water. Let the mixture bubble. Mix the cornflour mixture well, pour it into the wok, stirring, and simmer until the sauce thickens. Sprinkle the chilli over the beef and serve.

Nutritional information per portion: Energy 370kcal/1536kJ; Protein 25.5g; Carbohydrate 2.6g, of which sugars 2.4g; Fat 28.7g, of which saturates 7.2g; Cholesterol 69mg; Calcium 19mg; Fibre 0.9g; Sodium 588mg.

Beef with peppers and black bean sauce

A spicy, rich dish with the distinctive taste of black bean sauce. This is a recipe that will quickly become a favourite because it is so easy to prepare and quick to cook.

SERVES 4

350g/12oz rump (round) steak, trimmed
    and thinly sliced
20ml/4 tsp vegetable oil
300ml/½ pint/1¼ cups beef stock
2 garlic cloves, finely chopped
5ml/1 tsp grated fresh root ginger
1 fresh red chilli, seeded and finely chopped
15ml/1 tbsp black bean sauce
1 green (bell) pepper, seeded and
    cut into 2.5cm/1in squares
15ml/1 tbsp dry sherry
5ml/1 tsp cornflour (cornstarch)
5ml/1 tsp sugar
45ml/3 tbsp cold water
salt
cooked rice noodles, to serve

1 Place the steak in a bowl. Add 5ml/1 tsp of the oil and stir to coat.

2 Bring the stock to the boil in a pan. Add the beef and cook for 2 minutes, stirring constantly. Drain the beef and set aside. Retain the stock for use in another recipe.

3 Heat the remaining oil in a wok. Stir-fry the garlic, ginger and chilli with the black bean sauce for a few seconds.

4 Add the pepper squares and a little water to the wok. Cook for about 2 minutes more, then stir in the sherry. Add the beef slices to the pan, spoon the sauce over and reheat.

5 Mix the cornflour and sugar to a cream with the water. Pour the mixture into the pan. Cook, stirring, until the sauce has thickened. Season with salt. Transfer to warmed bowls and serve immediately, with rice noodles.

Nutritional information per portion: Energy 219kcal/912kJ; Protein 19.5g; Carbohydrate 8.4g, of which sugars 5.8g; Fat 12g, of which saturates 3.1g; Cholesterol 33mg; Calcium 69mg; Fibre 4.5g; Sodium 907mg.

Stir-fried beef in oyster sauce

*This simple recipe is often made with just straw mushrooms, which are available fresh in China,
but oyster mushrooms make a good substitute and using a mixture makes the dish extra interesting.*

SERVES 4–6

450g/1lb rump (round) steak
30ml/2 tbsp soy sauce
15ml/1 tbsp cornflour (cornstarch)
45ml/3 tbsp vegetable oil
15ml/1 tbsp chopped garlic
15ml/1 tbsp chopped fresh root ginger
225g/8oz/3¼ cups mixed mushrooms
  such as shiitake, oyster and straw
30ml/2 tbsp oyster sauce
5ml/1 tsp sugar
4 spring onions (scallions), cut into
  short lengths
ground black pepper
2 fresh red chillies, seeded and cut into
  strips, to garnish

1 Place the steak in the freezer for 30 minutes, until firm, then slice it on the diagonal into long thin strips.

2 Mix the soy sauce and cornflour in a large bowl. Add the steak, cover with clear film (plastic wrap) and leave at room temperature for 1–2 hours.

3 Heat half the oil in a wok. Add the garlic and ginger and cook for 1–2 minutes. Drain the steak, add it to the wok and stir well. Stir-fry for 2 minutes, until the steak is browned. Remove from the wok and set aside.

4 Heat the remaining oil in the wok. Add all of the mushrooms and stir-fry over a medium heat until golden brown.

5 Return the steak to the wok. Spoon in the oyster sauce and sugar, mix well, then add pepper to taste. Toss over the heat until all of the ingredients are thoroughly combined.

6 Stir in the spring onions. Transfer the mixture on to a serving platter, garnish with the strips of red chilli and serve.

Nutritional information per portion: Energy 171kcal/717kJ; Protein20g; Carbohydrate 8.3g, of which sugars 5.6g;
Fat 6.6g, of which saturates 1.9g; Cholesterol 52mg; Calcium 28mg; Fibre 1.1g; Sodium 343mg.

Vegetarian & vegetable dishes

The Chinese larder is laden with fresh

and exciting vegetables, as well as tofu

products that provide healthy protein

in a vegetarian diet. The dishes

featured in this chapter include

delicious vegetable main courses as

well as delectable side dishes such

as Mixed Stir-fry with Peanut Sauce,

Fried Garlic Tofu and Sesame-tossed

Asparagus with Bean Thread Noodles.

Stir-fried spicy aubergine

This dish is believed to have come from the Chinese province of Hunan, where the sauce used here, called dou banjiang, is popular. It is a bean paste infused with Sichuan peppercorns and chillies.

SERVES 4

2 large aubergines (eggplants)
30ml/2 tbsp vegetable oil
2 garlic cloves, crushed
30ml/2 tbsp chilli bean paste
    (dou banjiang)
200ml/7fl oz/scant 1 cup water
30ml/2 tbsp sesame oil
5ml/1 tsp sugar
rice or noodles, to serve

COOK'S TIP

To make dou banjiang, blend 60ml/4 tbsp yellow bean sauce with 15ml/1 tbsp chilli sauce, 5ml/1 tsp ground Sichuan peppercorns and 30ml/2 tbsp sesame oil.

1 Slice the aubergines in quarters lengthways then cut them across the grain into small chunks. Bring a large pan of water to the boil and blanch the aubergines for 3 minutes, then drain thoroughly.

2 Heat the oil in a wok or frying pan and stir-fry the garlic for 2 minutes. Add the chilli bean paste and cook rapidly for 1 minute, stirring.

3 Add the aubergines and stir-fry for 2 minutes. Add the water and bring to a fast boil. Simmer for 4 minutes until the sauce has thickened a little.

4 Add the sesame oil and stir for 30 seconds. Season with sugar to taste, and serve the dish piping hot with rice or noodles.

Nutritional information per portion: Energy 121kcal/501kJ; Protein 1g; Carbohydrate 3.9g, of which sugars 3.4g; Fat 11.6g, of which saturates 1.6g; Cholesterol 0mg; Calcium 12mg; Fibre 2g; Sodium 73mg.

Stir-fried Chinese broccoli

There was a time when this popular Chinese vegetable was practically unobtainable outside its country of origin, but airfreight has changed all that and most Chinese food stores now stock it.

SERVES 4

350g/12oz Chinese broccoli (kai lan)
30ml/2 tbsp vegetable oil
30ml/2 tbsp shredded fresh
   root ginger
30ml/2 tbsp crushed garlic
30ml/2 tbsp oyster sauce
30ml/2 tbsp rice wine

VARIATION

Tenderstem broccoli, now available in most supermarkets, comes close to Chinese broccoli in flavour and texture. Purple sprouting broccoli or chard can be used as a substitute.

1 Separate the kai lan leaves from the stalks. Cut each leaf in half. Trim the stalks, then peel them thinly, removing any tough portions of outer skin. Slice each stalk diagonally in half.

2 Bring a pan of water to the boil and blanch the kai lan leaves for 1 minute. Drain immediately in a colander, and refresh under cold water. This will help to retain the vegetable's bright green colour. Drain well. Repeat the process with the kai lan stalks, keeping leaves and stalks separate.

3 Heat the oil in a wok and fry the ginger and garlic until the latter is golden brown. Add the kai lan stalks and stir-fry for 1 minute. Add the leaves, stir well, then add the oyster sauce and wine. Stir rapidly over the heat for 2 minutes, spoon into a dish and serve immediately.

Nutritional Information per portion: Energy 103kcal/444kJ; Protein 5g; Carbohydrate 5.9g, of which sugars 3.7g; Fat 6.4g, of which saturates 0.8g; Cholesterol 0mg; Calcium 53mg; Fibre 2.9g; Sodium 131mg.

Stir-fried Chinese leaves

This simple way of cooking Chinese leaves preserves their delicate flavour. This dish makes an excellent accompaniment to main course meat and vegetable dishes.

SERVES 4

675g/1½lb Chinese leaves (Chinese cabbage)
15ml/1tbsp vegetable oil
2 garlic cloves, finely chopped
2.5cm/1in piece of fresh root ginger, finely chopped
2.5 ml/½ tsp salt
15ml/1 tbsp oyster sauce
4 spring onions (scallions), cut into 2.5cm/1in lengths

COOK'S TIP
If you are vegetarian, substitute 15ml/1 tbsp light soy sauce and 5ml/1 tsp of caster sugar for the oyster sauce.

1 Stack the Chinese leaves together and cut them into 2.5cm/1in slices.

2 Heat the oil in a wok or large pan. Stir-fry the garlic and ginger for 1 minute.

3 Add the Chinese leaves to the wok or pan and stir-fry for 2 minutes.

4 Sprinkle the salt over and drizzle with the oyster sauce. Toss the leaves over the heat for 2 minutes more.

5 Stir in the spring onions. Toss the mixture well to combine.

6 Transfer the leaves to a heated serving plate and serve.

Nutritional information per portion: Energy 77kcal/321kJ; Protein 2.6g; Carbohydrate 9.8g, of which sugars 9.6g; Fat 3.2g, of which saturates 0.3g; Cholesterol 0mg; Calcium 87mg; Fibre 3.7g; Sodium 74mg.

Hot lettuce with conpoy sauce

The Chinese rarely eat vegetables raw, even when using the most tender salad-type greens. Stir-frying them with aromatics like garlic and ginger is popular, and provides a tasty sauce.

SERVES 4

4 pieces conpoy (see Cook's tip)
200ml/7fl oz/scant 1 cup warm water
2 heads cos or romaine lettuce
15ml/1 tbsp vegetable oil
15ml/1 tbsp chopped fresh root ginger
2 garlic cloves, chopped
30ml/2 tbsp rice wine

COOK'S TIP

Conpoy is an expensive shellfish closely related to the scallop. It is only available dried and is used as a seasoning in a variety of dishes.

1 Put the pieces of conpoy in a bowl and pour over the warm water. Soak for 2–3 hours until soft. Meanwhile, shred the lettuce, put in a colander and rinse it under cold water. Drain well, then dry the lettuce thoroughly in a clean dish towel.

2 Drain the conpoy, reserving the soaking liquid. Use a sharp knife to shred the pieces finely.

3 Heat the oil in a wok and fry the ginger and garlic for 40 seconds, until light brown. Add the lettuce and stir-fry over high heat for 1 minute.

4 Add the conpoy, with the reserved soaking liquid and the rice wine. Bring to the boil and cook, stirring constantly, for 2 minutes. Transfer to a serving dish and serve immediately.

Nutritional information per portion: Energy 131kcal/549kJ; Protein 12.4g; Carbohydrate 3.5g, of which sugars 1.8g; Fat 6.7g, of which saturates 1g; Cholesterol 24mg; Calcium 43mg; Fibre 0.9g; Sodium 94mg.

Mixed stir-fry with peanut sauce

Wherever you go in China, stir-fried vegetables will be on the menu. This version, which is packed with vegetables and served with a spicy peanut sauce, makes a delicious vegetarian main course.

SERVES 4

6 dried Chinese mushrooms
20 dried tiger lily buds
60ml/4 tbsp sesame oil
225g/8oz tofu, sliced
1 large onion, finely sliced
1 large carrot, finely sliced
300g/11oz pak choi (bok choy),
    leaves separated from stems
225g/8oz can bamboo shoots, rinsed
50ml/2fl oz/¼ cup soy sauce
10ml/2 tsp sugar

FOR THE PEANUT SAUCE

15ml/1 tbsp sesame oil
2 garlic cloves, finely chopped
2 fresh red chillies, seeded and
    chopped
90g/3½oz/scant 1 cup unsalted roasted
    peanuts, finely chopped
150ml/5fl oz/⅔ cup coconut milk
30ml/2 tbsp hoisin sauce
15ml/1 tbsp soy sauce
15ml/1 tbsp sugar

1 Soak the dried mushrooms and lily buds in warm water for 20 minutes.

2 Meanwhile, make the sauce. Heat the oil in a wok and stir-fry the garlic and chillies until they begin to colour, then add almost all of the peanuts. Stir-fry for 2–3 minutes, then add the remaining ingredients. Bring to the boil, then simmer until thickened. Keep warm.

3 Drain the mushrooms and lily buds and squeeze out any excess water. Cut the mushroom caps into strips and discard the stalks. Trim off the hard ends of the lily buds and tie a knot in the centre of each one.

4 Heat 30ml/2 tbsp of the oil in a wok and brown the tofu on both sides. Drain and cut it into strips.

5 Heat the remaining oil in the wok and stir-fry the onion, carrot and pak choi stems for 2 minutes. Add the mushrooms, lily buds, tofu and bamboo shoots and stir-fry for 1 minute more.

6 Add the pak choi leaves, soy sauce and sugar to the wok and toss. Stir-fry until heated through.

7 Garnish with the remaining chopped peanuts and serve with the peanut sauce.

Nutritional information per portion: Energy 157kcal/656kJ; Protein 5.5g; Carbohydrate 13g, of which sugars 11.4g; Fat 9.6g, of which saturates 2.1g; Cholesterol 0mg; Calcium 110mg; Fibre 5.5g; Sodium 65mg.

Stir-fried seeds and vegetables

The contrast between the crunchy seeds and vegetables and the rich, savoury sauce is what makes this dish so delicious. Serve it on its own, or with rice or noodles.

SERVES 4

30ml/2 tbsp vegetable oil
30ml/2 tbsp sesame seeds
30ml/2 tbsp sunflower seeds
30ml/2 tbsp pumpkin seeds
2 garlic cloves, finely chopped
2.5cm/1in piece fresh root ginger, peeled and finely chopped
2 large carrots, cut into batons
2 courgettes (zucchini), cut into batons
90g/3^1/2oz/1^1/2 cups oyster mushrooms, torn In pieces
130g/3oz spinach leaves, coarsely chopped
a small bunch of fresh mint leaves
60ml/4 tbsp black bean sauce
30ml/2 tbsp light soy sauce
15ml/1 tbsp palm sugar (jaggery)
30ml/2 tbsp rice vinegar
rice or noodles, to serve (optional)

1 Heat the oil in a wok. Add the seeds. Toss over a medium heat for 1 minute, then add the garlic and ginger and stir-fry until the ginger is aromatic and the garlic is golden.

2 Add the carrots, courgettes and sliced oyster mushrooms to the wok and stir-fry over a medium heat for 5 minutes, until golden.

3 Add the spinach with the mint leaves. Toss over the heat for 1 minute, then stir in the black bean sauce, soy sauce, sugar and vinegar.

4 Stir-fry for a further 1–2 minutes, until thoroughly combined and heated through. Transfer the stir-fry to warmed bowls and serve on its own, or with rice or noodles.

Nutritional information per portion: Energy 205kcal/849kJ; Protein 6.9g; Carbohydrate 9.7g, of which sugars 7.7g; Fat 15.6g, of which saturates 2g; Cholesterol 0mg; Calcium 159mg; Fibre 3.4g; Sodium 294mg.

Sweet and sour vegetables with tofu

This is a colourful dish that will be popular with vegetarians and meat-eaters alike. Stir-fries are always a good choice when entertaining, because you can prepare the ingredients ahead of time and then cook them incredibly quickly in the wok.

SERVES 4

4 shallots

3 garlic cloves

30ml/2 tbsp groundnut (peanut) oil

250g/9oz Chinese leaves (Chinese cabbage), shredded

8 baby corn cobs, sliced on the diagonal

2 red (bell) peppers, seeded and thinly sliced

200g/7oz/1³⁄₄ cups mangetouts (snow peas), trimmed and sliced

250g/9oz tofu, rinsed, drained and cut in 1cm/¹⁄₂in cubes

60ml/4 tbsp vegetable stock

30ml/2 tbsp light soy sauce

15ml/1 tbsp sugar

30ml/2 tbsp rice vinegar

2.5ml/¹⁄₂ tsp dried chilli flakes

small bunch of coriander (cilantro), chopped

1 Slice the shallots thinly using a sharp knife. Finely chop the garlic.

2 Heat the oil in a wok or large frying pan and cook the shallots and garlic for 2–3 minutes over a medium heat, until golden. Do not let the garlic burn or it will taste bitter.

3 Add the shredded Chinese leaves, toss over the heat for 30 seconds, then add the sliced baby corn cobs and repeat the process.

4 Add the red peppers, mangetouts and tofu in the same way, each time adding a single ingredient and tossing it over the heat for about 30 seconds before adding the next.

5 Pour in the stock and soy sauce. Mix together the sugar and vinegar in a small bowl, stirring until the sugar has dissolved, then add to the wok or pan. Sprinkle over the chilli flakes and coriander, toss to mix well and serve.

Nutritional information per portion: Energy 180Kcal/751kJ; Protein 9.1g; Carbohydrate 17g, of which sugars 15.6g; Fat 8.7g, of which saturates 1.1g; Cholesterol 0mg; Calcium 386mg; Fibre 4.1g; Sodium 575mg.

Mixed vegetables monk-style

Chinese monks eat neither meat nor fish, so "monk-style" dishes are perfect for vegetarians. Fresh lotus root should be available in Chinese supermarkets, but you can use the canned variety.

SERVES 4

50g/2oz dried tofu sticks, soaked in hot water for 1 hour

10g/¹/₄oz dried cloud ears (wood ears), soaked in hot water for 15 minutes

8 dried Chinese mushrooms, soaked in hot water for 15 minutes

15ml/1tbsp vegetable oil

115g/4oz lotus root, peeled and sliced

75g/3oz/³/₄ cup drained, canned straw mushrooms

115g/4oz/1 cup baby corn cobs, cut in half

30ml/2tbsp light soy sauce

15ml/1tbsp dry sherry

10ml/2tsp caster (superfine) sugar

150ml/¹/₄ pint/²/₃ cup vegetable stock

75g/3oz mangetouts (snowpeas), cut in half

5ml/1tsp cornflour (cornstarch)

15ml/1tbsp cold water

1 Drain the cloud ears, trim off and discard the hard base from each and cut the rest into bitesize pieces. Drain the soaked mushrooms, trim off and discard the stems and chop the caps roughly.

2 Drain the tofu sticks. Cut them into 5cm/2in long pieces, discarding any hard pieces.

3 Heat the oil in a non-stick frying pan or wok. Stir-fry the cloud ears, dried Chinese mushrooms and lotus root for about 30 seconds.

4 Add the pieces of tofu sticks, straw mushrooms, baby corn cobs, soy sauce, sherry, caster sugar and stock. Bring to the boil, then cover the pan or wok, lower the heat and simmer for about 20 minutes.

5 Stir in the mangetouts and cook, uncovered, for 2 minutes more. Mix the cornflour to a paste with the water. Add the mixture to the pan or wok. Cook, stirring, until the sauce thickens. Transfer to warmed bowls and serve at once.

Nutritional information per portion: Energy 95kcal/399kJ; Protein 3.3g; Carbohydrate 12g, of which sugars 4.6g; Fat 3.6g, of which saturates 0.4g; Cholesterol 0mg; Calcium 91mg; Fibre 1.4g; Sodium 885mg.

Fried garlic tofu

A simple and inexpensive recipe that can be quickly and easily prepared to make a tasty and nutritious midweek family supper. Serve with mixed salad leaves or steamed greens.

SERVES 4

500g/1¼lb firm tofu
50g/2oz/¼ cup butter
2 garlic cloves, thinly sliced
200g/7oz enoki or other mushrooms
45ml/3 tbsp soy sauce
30ml/2 tbsp rice wine

COOK'S TIP
Enoki mushrooms are slender and extremely delicate, with long thin stems and tiny white caps. They have a sweet, almost fruity flavour.

1 Wrap the tofu in kitchen paper, place a weighted plate on top and leave for up to 1 hour to drain off excess water.

2 Slice the tofu to make 16 slices using a sharp knife.

3 Melt one-third of the butter in a heavy frying pan. Add the garlic and cook over a medium heat, stirring, until golden, but do not allow it to burn. Remove the garlic from the pan.

4 Melt half the remaining butter in the pan, add the mushrooms and cook for 4 minutes, until golden, then remove from the pan.

5 Place the tofu in the pan with the remaining butter and cook until golden. Flip and cook the other side until golden and warmed through.

6 Return the garlic to the pan, add the soy sauce and rice wine and simmer for 1 minute. Serve with the mushrooms.

Nutritional information per portion: Energy 196kcal/810kJ; Protein 11.5g; Carbohydrate 2.1g, of which sugars 1.4g; Fat 15.8g, of which saturates 7.2g; Cholesterol 27mg; Calcium 645mg; Fibre 0.6g; Sodium 884mg.

Stir-fried crispy tofu

The asparagus grown in the part of China where this recipe originated tends to have slender stalks. Look for it in Thai markets or substitute the thin asparagus popularly known as sprue.

SERVES 2

250g/9oz fried tofu cubes
30ml/2 tbsp groundnut (peanut) oil
15ml/1 tbsp green curry paste
30ml/2 tbsp light soy sauce
2 kaffir lime leaves, rolled into cylinders
   and thinly sliced
30ml/2 tbsp sugar
150ml/¼ pint/⅔ cup vegetable stock
250g/9oz Asian asparagus, trimmed and
   sliced into 5cm/2in lengths
30ml/2 tbsp roasted peanuts, finely
   chopped

1 Preheat the grill (broiler) to medium. Place the tofu cubes in a grill pan and grill (broil) for 2–3 minutes, then turn them over and cook until they are crisp and golden brown all over.

2 Heat the oil in a wok. Add the green curry paste and cook over a medium heat, stirring constantly, for 1–2 minutes, until it gives off its aroma.

3 Stir the soy sauce, lime leaves, sugar and vegetable stock into the wok and mix well. Bring to the boil, then reduce the heat to a simmer.

4 Add the asparagus and simmer for 5 minutes. Quarter each piece of tofu, then add to the wok with the peanuts.

5 Toss to coat all the ingredients in the sauce, then spoon into a warmed dish and serve immediately.

Nutritional information per portion: Energy 287kcal/1195kJ; Protein 14.3g; Carbohydrate 20.3g, of which sugars 19.5g; Fat 17g, of which saturates 2.1g; Cholesterol 0mg; Calcium 682mg; Fibre 2.1g; Sodium 1075mg

Chinese chives and tofu stir-fry

These chives are different from the variety used as a herb in the West, being thicker and with a more pronounced aroma. In traditional Chinese medicine they are valued for their blood-purifying properties and are purported to alleviate impotence – a good reason to eat a whole plateful.

SERVES 4

275g/10oz Chinese chives
8 pieces of firm tofu, 7.5cm/3in square
    and 4cm/1½in thick
30ml/2 tbsp vegetable oil
2 garlic cloves, crushed
30ml/2 tbsp light soy sauce
90ml/3 fl oz/¼ cup water

COOK'S TIP

Chinese or garlic chives are now widely available in supermarkets as well as in Asian markets. Both the leaves and the flower stems can be used.

1 Cut the chives into 7.5cm/3in lengths, wash and drain. Remove any that are tired-looking.

2 Cut each piece of tofu into four. Heat the oil in a wok or large frying pan and fry them lightly until just brown and warmed through.

3 Push the tofu aside and fry the garlic until light brown, then add the chives.

4 Stir-fry rapidly over a high heat for 2 minutes. Add the soy sauce and water and stir for 2 minutes. Serve hot.

Nutritional information per portion: Energy 125kcal/516kJ; Protein 8.2g; Carbohydrate 2.3g, of which sugars 1.8g; Fat 9.2g, of which saturates 1.1g; Cholesterol 0mg; Calcium 501mg; Fibre 1.5g; Sodium 633mg.

Sesame-tossed asparagus with bean thread noodles

Tender asparagus spears tossed with sesame seeds and served on a bed of crispy, deep-fried noodles makes a lovely dish for casual entertaining. The lightly cooked asparagus retains all its fresh flavour and bite, which contrasts wonderfully with the crunchy noodles.

SERVES 4

15ml/1 tbsp sunflower oil
350g/12oz thin asparagus spears
5ml/1 tsp salt
5ml/1 tsp ground black pepper
5ml/1 tsp golden caster (superfine) sugar
30ml/2 tbsp rice wine
45ml/3 tbsp light soy sauce
60ml/4 tbsp oyster sauce
10ml/2 tsp sesame oil
60ml/4 tbsp toasted sesame seeds

FOR THE NOODLES

50g/2oz dried bean thread noodles
   or thin rice noodles
sunflower oil, for frying

1 First make the crispy noodles. Fill a wok one-third full of oil and heat to 180°C/350°F (or until a cube of bread, dropped into the oil, browns in 40 seconds). Add the noodles, small bunches at a time, to the oil; they will crisp and puff up in seconds. Drain on kitchen paper. Set aside.

2 Heat a clean wok over a high heat and add the sunflower oil. Add the asparagus and stir-fry for 3 minutes.

3 Add the salt, pepper, sugar, wine and both sauces to the wok and stir-fry for 2–3 minutes. Add the sesame oil, toss to combine and remove from the heat.

4 Divide the noodles between four warmed plates or bowls and top with the asparagus and juices. Sprinkle over the sesame seeds and serve immediately.

Nutritional information per portion: Energy 131kcal/547kJ; Protein 4.6g; Carbohydrate 16.5g, of which sugars 6.9g; Fat 5.6g, of which saturates 0.6g; Cholesterol 0mg; Calcium 31mg; Fibre 2g; Sodium 1047mg.

Marinated tofu and broccoli with crispy fried shallots

Meltingly tender tofu flavoured with a fragrant blend of spices and served with tender young stems of broccoli makes a perfect light supper or lunch. You can buy the crispy fried shallots from Asian supermarkets, but they are very easy to make yourself.

SERVES 6

500g/1¼lb block of firm tofu, drained
45ml/3 tbsp kecap manis
30ml/2 tbsp sweet chilli sauce
45ml/3 tbsp soy sauce
5ml/1 tsp sesame oil
5ml/1 tsp finely grated fresh
   root ginger

400g/14oz tenderstem broccoli,
   halved lengthways
45ml/3 tbsp roughly chopped
   coriander (cilantro)
30ml/2 tbsp toasted sesame seeds
30ml/2 tbsp crispy fried shallots
steamed rice or noodles, to serve

1 Cut the tofu into four triangular pieces: slice the block in half widthways, then diagonally. Place in a heatproof dish.

2 In a small bowl, combine the kecap manis, chilli sauce, soy sauce, sesame oil and ginger, then pour over the tofu. Leave the tofu to marinate for at least 30 minutes, turning occasionally.

3 Place the broccoli on a heatproof plate and place on a trivet or steamer rack in the wok. Cover and steam for 4–5 minutes, until just tender. Remove and keep warm.

4 Place the dish of tofu on the trivet or steamer rack in the wok, cover and steam for 4–5 minutes.

5 Divide the broccoli among four warmed serving plates and top each one with a piece of tofu.

6 Spoon the remaining juices over the tofu and broccoli, then sprinkle over the coriander, sesame seeds and crispy shallots. Serve immediately with steamed rice or noodles.

Nutritional information per portion: Energy 202kcal/840kJ; Protein 16.5g; Carbohydrate 6.9g, of which sugars 5.6g; Fat 12.1g, of which saturates 1.7g; Cholesterol 0mg; Calcium 750mg; Fibre 3.5g; Sodium 938mg.

Broccoli with soy sauce

A wonderfully simple dish that you will want to make again and again. The broccoli cooks in next to no time, so don't start cooking until you are almost ready to eat.

SERVES 4

450g/1lb broccoli
15ml/1 tbsp vegetable oil
2 garlic cloves, sliced
30ml/2tbsp light soy sauce
salt

COOK'S TIP
Broccoli is a rich source of vitamin C, folic acid and several other important nutrients and antioxidants.

VARIATIONS
Cos lettuce or Chinese leaves (Chinese cabbage) are delicious prepared this way.

1 Trim the thick stems of the broccoli and cut the head into large florets.

2 Bring a pan of lightly salted water to the boil. Add the broccoli and cook for 3–4 minutes until crisp-tender.

3 Drain the broccoli thoroughly and transfer it to a heated serving dish.

4 Heat the oil in a small pan. Fry the sliced garlic for 2 minutes to release the flavour, then remove it with a slotted spoon. Pour the oil carefully over the broccoli, taking care as it will splatter.

5 Drizzle the soy sauce over the broccoli, sprinkle over the fried garlic and serve immediately.

Nutritional information per portion: Energy 65kcal/271kJ; Protein 5.2g; Carbohydrate 2.7g, of which sugars 2.2g; Fat 3.8g, of which saturates 0.6g; Cholesterol 0mg; Calcium 64mg; Fibre 2.9g; Sodium 543mg.

Broccoli with sesame seeds

This simple treatment is ideal for broccoli and other brassicas, including Brussels sprouts. Adding a sprinkling of toasted sesame seeds is an inspired touch.

SERVES 2

225g/8oz purple sprouting broccoli
15ml/1 tbsp vegetable oil
15ml/1 tbsp soy sauce
15ml/1 tbsp toasted sesame seeds
salt and ground black pepper

VARIATIONS

• Sprouting broccoli has been used for this recipe, but when it is not available an ordinary variety of broccoli, such as calabrese, will also work very well.
• An even better choice would be Chinese broccoli, which is often available in Asian markets under the name kai lan.

1 Using a sharp knife, cut off and discard any thick stems from the broccoli and cut the broccoli into long, thin florets. Stems that are young and tender can be sliced into rounds.

2 Remove any bruised or discoloured portions of the stem along with any florets that are no longer firm and tightly curled.

3 Heat the vegetable oil in a wok or large frying pan and add the broccoli. Stir-fry for 3–4 minutes, or until tender, adding a splash of water if the pan becomes too dry.

4 Mix the soy sauce with the sesame seeds, then season with salt and ground black pepper. Add to the broccoli and toss to combine. Transfer to a serving platter and serve immediately.

Nutritional information per portion: Energy 135kcal/558kJ; Protein 6.6g; Carbohydrate 2.7g, of which sugars 2.3g; Fat 10.9g, of which saturates 1.5g; Cholesterol 0mg; Calcium 115mg; Fibre 3.5g; Sodium 545mg.

Broccoli and mushroom salad with tofu

*This bold-flavoured salad combines satisfyingly contrasting textures in the tofu and vegetables.
It could be served with rice and a pinch of dried chilli flakes to make a delicious meal.*

SERVES 4–6

250g/9oz firm tofu, drained and cubed
250g/9oz broccoli, cut into large florets
15ml/1 tbsp olive oil
1 garlic clove, finely chopped
350g/12oz chestnut mushrooms, sliced
4 spring onions (scallions), thinly sliced
75g/3oz/³⁄₄ cup pine nuts, toasted

FOR THE MARINADE

1 garlic clove, crushed
2.5cm/1in piece fresh root ginger, grated
45ml/3 tbsp soy sauce
45ml/3 tbsp tamari soy sauce
45ml/3 tbsp rice wine
1.5ml/¹⁄₄ tsp cumin seeds, toasted and
    coarsely crushed
1.5ml/¹⁄₄ tsp caster (superfine) sugar
ground black pepper

1 Mix all the marinade ingredients together. Place the tofu cubes in a bowl, pour in the marinade, toss to coat and leave for at least 1 hour.

2 Meanwhile, steam the broccoli for 4–5 minutes, until tender, then refresh under cold running water.

3 Heat the oil in a wok. Add the garlic and stir-fry over a low heat for 1 minute, until golden.

4 Add the mushrooms and fry over a high heat for 5 minutes, until cooked through. Add the broccoli to the wok and season with ground black pepper.

5 Toss the tofu and its marinade into the wok with the broccoli, mushrooms and spring onions.

6 Sprinkle with the pine nuts and serve immediately.

Nutritional information per portion: Energy 148kcal/6141kJ; Protein 9g; Carbohydrate 4g, of which sugars 3g; Fat 11g, of which saturates 1g; Cholesterol 0mg; Calcium 248mg; Fibre 1.5g; Sodium 1077mg.

Mushrooms and bamboo shoots in yellow bean sauce

Yellow bean sauce has a lovely, nutty tang that blends well with most ingredients. The mushrooms can be Chinese dried ceps, fresh shiitake or field mushrooms, or several different types.

SERVES 4–6

150g/5oz mushrooms, any type, soaked
    until soft if dried
150g/5oz canned bamboo shoots
30ml/2 tbsp vegetable oil
2 spring onions (scallions), chopped
30ml/2 tbsp yellow bean sauce
5ml/1 tsp sugar
175ml/6fl oz/¾ cup water
5ml/1 tsp cornflour (cornstarch),
    blended with a little water
30ml/2 tbsp sesame oil

1 Cut each mushroom in half. Drain the bamboo shoots and rinse under cold running water, then drain again and cut into slices.

2 Heat the oil in a wok or large, heavy pan and fry the spring onions for 1 minute. Add the yellow bean sauce and fry for 1 minute.

3 Add the mushrooms and sliced bamboo shoots. Stir-fry over a high heat for about 2 minutes.

4 Add the sugar, water and cornflour blended with a little water. Stir for another minute. Add the sesame oil, stir rapidly for 1 minute more and serve at once.

Nutritional information per portion: Energy 83kcal/346kJ; Protein 2.4g; Carbohydrate 5.3g, of which sugars 2.4g; Fat 6g, of which saturates 0.7g; Cholesterol 0mg; Calcium 18mg; Fibre 1.5g; Sodium 34mg.

Braised tofu with mushrooms

Four different kinds of mushrooms combine beautifully with tofu in this recipe. Chinese flavourings enhance all the ingredients to make this the perfect vegetarian side dish to serve at a dinner party.

SERVES 4

350g/12oz firm tofu
2.5ml/¹/₂ tsp sesame oil
10ml/2 tsp light soy sauce
15ml/1 tbsp vegetable oil
2 garlic cloves, finely chopped
2.5ml/¹/₂ tsp grated fresh root ginger
115g/4oz/scant 2 cups fresh shiitake
    mushrooms, stalks removed
175g/6oz/scant 2 cups fresh
    oyster mushrooms

115g/4oz/scant 2 cups drained, canned
    straw mushrooms
115g/4oz/scant 2 cups button (white) mushrooms, halved
15ml/1 tbsp rice wine or dry sherry
15ml/1 tbsp dark soy sauce
90ml/6 tbsp vegetable stock
5ml/1 tsp cornflour (cornstarch)
15ml/1 tbsp cold water
salt and ground white pepper
2 shredded spring onions (scallions), to garnish

1 Put the tofu in a dish or bowl and sprinkle with the sesame oil, light soy sauce and a large pinch of pepper. Leave to marinate for 10 minutes, then drain and cut into 2.5 x 1cm/1 x ¹/₂in pieces using a sharp knife.

2 Heat the vegetable oil in a large non-stick frying pan or wok. When the oil is very hot, add the garlic and ginger and stir-fry for a few seconds. Add all the mushrooms and stir-fry for a further 2 minutes.

3 Stir in the rice wine or dry sherry, dark soy sauce and stock. Season to taste with salt, if necessary, and ground white pepper. Lower the heat and simmer gently for 4 minutes.

4 Place the cornflour in a bowl with the water. Mix to make a smooth paste. Stir the cornflour mixture into the pan or wok and cook, stirring constantly to prevent lumps, until thickened.

5 Carefully add the pieces of tofu, toss gently to coat thoroughly in the sauce and simmer for about 2 minutes.

6 Transfer to a warm serving dish or individual plates, sprinkle the shredded spring onions over the top, and serve immediately.

Nutritional information per portion: Energy 118kcal/490kJ; Protein 8.2g; Carbohydrate 14g, of which sugars 8.8g; Fat 3.7g, of which saturates 0.4g; Cholesterol 0mg; Calcium 385mg; Fibre 1.9g; Sodium 1076mg.

Chinese steamed winter melon with barley

To the Chinese, all parts of the winter melon, including the seeds, rind, pulp and juice, are regarded as good for the treatment of urinary and kidney diseases. In this recipe the skin of the melon could be scooped out and used as an attractive container for the soup.

SERVES 4–6

1 whole winter melon (about
   1.2kg/2½lb), halved
45ml/3 tbsp hulled or pearl barley,
   soaked in water for several hours, or
   boiled for 20 minutes
600ml/1 pint/2½ cups very
   hot water
15ml/1 tbsp preserved winter melon
   (tung chai)
5ml/1 tsp salt
15ml/1 tbsp sesame oil
ground black pepper

1 Remove the pith and seeds from the melon, then scoop out the flesh.

2 Place the melon in a deep bowl and place in a steamer that has a high-domed lid. Pour the hot water into the bowl and stir in the barley, salt and sesame oil. Cover the bowl, and steam for 30 minutes.

3 At the end of the cooking time the barley grains should be plump and very soft. Season to taste with black pepper.

4 Serve the winter melon and barley in its steaming dish straight from the steamer, while still piping hot.

Nutritional information per portion: Energy 125kcal/529kJ; Protein 2.2g; Carbohydrate 23.4g, of which sugars 14g; Fat 3.2g, of which saturates 0.4g; Cholesterol 0mg; Calcium 35mg; Fibre 1g; Sodium 569mg.

Stir-fried bitter gourd with sambal

According to the principles of Chinese medicine, any food that has a bitter edge is good for cleansing the liver. Bitter gourd fulfils this role brilliantly. Its tanginess is appetizing as well as beneficial, and the piquant sambal enhances the taste greatly.

SERVES 4

1 whole bitter gourd
30ml/2 tbsp vegetable oil
30ml/2 tbsp sambal goreng
    (fried chilli paste)
100ml/3¹/₂fl oz/scant ¹/₂ cup water
5ml/1 tsp sugar
15ml/1 tbsp lime juice

1 Cut the bitter gourd in half down its length. Use a spoon to scoop out the pith and red seeds. Slice into half moon pieces each 1cm/¹/₂in wide.

2 Bring a pan of water to the boil and blanch the bitter gourd for 2 minutes. Drain. This removes some bitterness and shortens the cooking time.

3 Heat the oil and fry the sambal goreng for just 1 minute, as it is already cooked. Add the pieces of gourd and stir-fry rapidly for 3 minutes.

4 Add the water, sugar and lime juice and continue to stir for another 2 minutes until the ingredients are well blended. Serve hot.

Nutritional information per portion: Energy 72kcal/299kJ; Protein 1.3g; Carbohydrate 3.9g, of which sugars 3.3g; Fat 5.8g, of which saturates 0.8g; Cholesterol 0mg; Calcium 41mg; Fibre 1.3g; Sodium 1mg.

Desserts

China is not as famous for its desserts

as for many of its other culinary

delicacies, but there is a myriad of

sweet Chinese treats that deserve to be

better known. Among the many

sumptuous and authentic options

sampled in this chapter are a subtly

sweet Almond Jelly, sweet and crunchy

Chinese Toffee Apples, and surprisingly

traditional Egg Tarts.

Almond jelly

This dish from Hong Kong is traditionally made using soaked, ground whole almonds. This simplified version, using almond extract, requires less effort and gives results that are just as good. The jelly has a subtle, sweet flavour that is popular with children and adults alike.

SERVES 6-8

750ml/1¼ pints/3 cups cold water
25g/1oz agar agar strips
15ml/1 tbsp powdered gelatine
300g/10oz/1½ cups sugar
150ml/¼ pint/²⁄₃ cup evaporated milk
15ml/1 tbsp almond extract
fruit cocktail or lychees, to serve

VARIATIONS
The flavour of almond is not to everyone's taste. Use vanilla as a substitute. Evaporated milk gives the jelly an opaque appearance; use water alone if you prefer a translucent jelly.

1 Pour the cold water into a pan and add the agar agar strips. Sprinkle the gelatine on the surface. Heat gently, stirring until all the agar agar and gelatine has dissolved.

2 Add the sugar. Simmer, stirring constantly, until the sugar has dissolved, then stir in the evaporated milk and almond extract.

3 Rinse a jelly mould with cold water and stand it upside down to drain. Stir the almond mixture well, then pour it into the jelly mould. Leave to cool, then chill until set.

4 Loosen the sides of the jelly with a knife, then unmould it on to a serving plate. If it is reluctant to leave the mould, dip it briefly in warm water before trying again. Serve with fruit cocktail or lychees.

Nutritional information per portion: Energy 181kcal/768kJ; Protein 4.8g; Carbohydrate 41.1g, of which sugars 41.1g; Fat 0.8g, of which saturates 0.5g; Cholesterol 3mg; Calcium 69mg; Fibre 0g; Sodium 24mg.

Lotus seeds in syrup

Within the pantheon of Chinese herbal remedies, lotus seeds are believed to aid blood circulation and stimulate sluggish appetites, while ginkgo nuts have for thousands of years been famed for their curative properties. Both turn up in herbal soups and sweet drinks like this one.

SERVES 4

750ml/1¹/₄ pints/3 cups water
100g/3³/₄oz rock sugar
40 drained canned lotus seeds
40 drained canned ginkgo nuts
6 pieces preserved sweet
   winter melon , cut in half

1 Put the water in a pan. Bring to the boil and add the rock sugar. Stir over the heat until it has dissolved.

2 Taste the syrup for sweetness and add more sugar if necessary. Stir in the lotus seeds and nuts with the preserved sweet winter melon. Simmer for 20 minutes. Serve hot or cold.

Nutritional information per portion: Energy 531kcal/2209kJ; Protein 5g; Carbohydrate 42.8g, of which sugars 42.4g; Fat 38.9g, of which saturates 5.6g; Cholesterol 0mg; Calcium 43mg; Fibre 3.4g; Sodium 143mg.

Caramelized plums with sticky coconut rice

Red, juicy plums are quickly seared in a wok with sugar to make a rich caramel coating, then served with sticky coconut-flavoured rice for a satisfying dessert. The glutinous rice is available from Asian stores, but remember that you have to soak it overnight before you start.

SERVES 4

6 or 8 firm, ripe plums
90g/3¹/₂oz/¹/₂ cup caster
  (superfine) sugar

FOR THE RICE

115g/4oz sticky glutinous rice
150ml/¹/₄ pint/²/₃ cup coconut cream
45ml/3 tbsp caster (superfine) sugar
a pinch of salt

1 First prepare the rice. Rinse it in several changes of water, then leave to soak overnight in a bowl of cold water.

2 Line a large bamboo steamer with muslin (cheesecloth). Drain the rice and spread out evenly on the muslin.

3 Cover the rice and steam over simmering water for 25–30 minutes, until the rice is tender. (Check the water level and add more if necessary.)

4 Transfer the steamed rice to a wide bowl and set aside.

5 Combine the coconut cream with the sugar and salt and pour into a clean wok. Heat gently and bring to the boil, then remove from the heat and pour over the rice. Stir to mix well.

6 Cut the plums in half and remove their stones (pits). Sprinkle the sugar over the cut sides.

7 Heat a non-stick wok over a medium-high heat. Working in batches, place the plums in the wok, cut side down, and cook for 1–2 minutes, or until the sugar caramelizes. (You might have to wipe out the wok with kitchen paper in between batches.)

8 Mould the rice into rounds and place on warmed plates, then spoon over the caramelized plums. Alternatively, simply spoon the rice into four warmed bowls and top with the plums.

Nutritional information per portion: Energy 298kcal/1265kJ; Protein 3.6g; Carbohydrate 71.7g, of which sugars 50.2g; Fat 0.7g, of which saturates 0.1g; Cholesterol 0mg; Calcium 53mg; Fibre 2.4g; Sodium 47mg.

Black glutinous rice pudding

Black glutinous rice has long dark grains and a nutty taste similar to wild rice. This baked pudding has a distinct character and flavour all of its own, as well as an intriguing appearance.

SERVES 4–6

175g/6oz/1 cup black or white
    glutinous rice
30ml/2 tbsp soft light brown sugar
475ml/16fl oz/2 cups coconut milk
250ml/8fl oz/1 cup water
3 eggs
30ml/2 tbsp sugar

COOK'S TIP
Black glutinous rice is usually used for sweet dishes, while its white counterpart is more often used in savoury recipes.

1 Combine the glutinous rice and brown sugar in a pan. Pour in half the coconut milk and the water.

2 Bring to the boil, reduce the heat to low and simmer, stirring occasionally, for 15–20 minutes, or until the rice has absorbed most of the liquid. Preheat the oven to 150°C/300°F/Gas 2.

3 Spoon the rice into a large ovenproof dish or individual ramekins.

4 Beat the eggs with the remaining coconut milk and sugar. Strain the egg mixture into a jug (pitcher), then pour it over the par-cooked rice.

5 Place the dish or ramekins in a roasting pan. Carefully pour in enough hot water to come halfway up the sides of the dish or ramekins.

6 Cover with foil and bake for about 35–60 minutes, or until the custard has set. Serve warm or cold.

Nutritional information per portion: Energy 135Kcal/568kJ; Protein 1.7g; Carbohydrate 31.8g, of which sugars 17.4g; Fat 0.3g, of which saturates 0g; Cholesterol 0mg; Calcium 247mg; Fibre 0g; Sodium 2mg.

Red bean pudding

Red aduki beans are used in many Chinese sweet dishes. At some of the hawker stalls, this pudding is presented on a banana leaf with a drizzle of coconut milk.

SERVES 4–6

115g/4oz dried red aduki beans, soaked in
    water for 2 hours
1.2 litres/2 pints/5 cups water
4 pandan (screwpine) leaves
150g/5oz/³/4 cup sugar
150ml/¼ pint /²/3 cup thick coconut
    milk, fresh or canned, beaten until
    smooth, or fresh coconut cream

1 Drain the soaked beans and put them in a deep pan. Add the water and bring it to the boil. Add the pandan leaves and reduce the heat.

2 Simmer, uncovered, for about 40 minutes until the beans are tender and the water has greatly reduced. Stir in the sugar.

3 Allow the sugar to dissolve, and simmer for a further 10 minutes.

4 Remove the pandan leaves and spoon the beans into individual bowls. Serve hot or leave to cool and chill before serving. Serve the coconut milk or cream separately, to pour over.

Nutritional information per portion: Energy 155kcal/661kJ; Protein 4.4g; Carbohydrate 35.8g, of which sugars 27.8g; Fat 0.4g, of which saturates 0.1g; Cholesterol 0mg; Calcium 40mg; Fibre 3g; Sodium 33mg.

Pancakes with red bean paste

In China, sweetened red beans are often used in desserts because the rich colour is associated with good luck. Here they are used as a delicious filling to moreishly sweet pancakes.

SERVES 4

600ml/1 pint/2¹/₂ cups cold water
175g/6oz/1 scant cup aduki beans,
   soaked overnight in cold water
115g/4oz/1 cup plain (all-purpose) flour
1 large (US extra large) egg, lightly beaten
300ml/¹/₂ pint/1¹/₄ cups semi-skimmed
   (low-fat) milk

5ml/1 tsp vegetable oil
75g/3oz/6 tbsp caster
   (superfine) sugar
2.5ml/¹/₂ tsp vanilla extract
fromage frais or natural
   (plain) yogurt,
   to serve (optional)

1 Bring the water to the boil in a pan. Drain the beans in a sieve (strainer), add them to the pan and boil rapidly for 10 minutes.

2 Skim off any scum from the surface of the liquid, then lower the heat, cover the pan and simmer, stirring occasionally, for 40 minutes or until the beans are soft.

3 Meanwhile, make the pancakes. Sift the flour into a bowl and make a well in the centre. Pour in the egg and half the milk. Beat, gradually drawing in the flour until it has all been incorporated. Beat in the remaining milk to make a smooth batter. Cover and set aside for 30 minutes.

4 Heat a 20cm/8in non-stick omelette pan and brush lightly with the vegetable oil. Pour in a little of the batter, swirling the pan to cover the base thinly.

5 Cook the pancake for 2 minutes until the bottom has browned lightly. Flip the pancake over, either with chopsticks or by flipping in the air, and cook the second side for about 1 minute. Slide the pancake on to a plate.

6 Make seven more pancakes in the same way. Cover the pancakes with foil and keep hot.

7 When the beans are soft and all the water has been absorbed, put them into a food processor and process until almost smooth. Add the sugar and vanilla extract and process briefly until the sugar has dissolved.

8 Preheat the grill (broiler). Spread a little of the bean paste on the centre of each pancake and fold them into parcels, pressing them down with your fingers to flatten.

9 Place on a baking sheet and cook under the grill for a few minutes until crisp and lightly toasted on each side.

10 Serve the hot pancakes immediately, either on their own or with a little fromage frais or natural yogurt.

Nutritional information per portion: Energy 368kcal/1562kJ; Protein 17.2g; Carbohydrate 69.1g, of which sugars 24.8g; Fat 4.5g, of which saturates 1.6g; Cholesterol 52mg; Calcium 183mg; Fibre 4.5g; Sodium 59mg.

Bean paste buns

There are scores of different dumplings in the dim sum repertoire. The dough for these is similar to many savoury dim sum dumplings, but the filling is a sweet bean paste called tau sa.

SERVES 12

200g/7oz/1³/₄ cups bun flour or
    self-raising (self-rising) flour
5ml/1 tsp sugar
a pinch of salt
15g/¹/₂oz easy-blend (rapid-rise)
    dried yeast
120ml/4fl oz/¹/₂ cup warm water
1 can sweet bean paste (about
    300g/11oz depending on the brand)

1 Put the flour, sugar, salt and yeast in a mixing bowl. Make a well in the centre and pour in the water. Mix to a dough. Knead the dough on a floured board for 10 minutes. Return it to the bowl, cover and set aside in a warm place to rise for 20 minutes.

2 Knock back (punch down) the dough, knead it again, return to the bowl and set aside for 15 minutes.

3 Roll out the dough on a floured board and shape it into a 30cm/ 12in roll about 5cm/2in in diameter. Cut into 2.5cm/1in slices and flatten each of these to a thin round, about 10cm/4in across.

4 Holding a pastry round on the palm of one hand, spoon a tablespoon of the filling into the centre. Cup your hand so that the dough enfolds the filling, pleating and pinching it where necessary. Pinch off any excess dough at the top and seal with a firm twisting action. It is important that the buns are properly sealed, otherwise they will gape when steamed. Repeat this process for the remaining dumplings.

5 Cut 5cm/2in squares of baking parchment. Stand a dumpling on each piece of paper in a steamer. Steam for 15 minutes. Serve immediately.

Nutritional information per portion: Energy 112kcal/477kJ; Protein 4.5g; Carbohydrate 24.1g, of which sugars 5g; Fat 0.4g, of which saturates 0.1g; Cholesterol 0mg; Calcium 36mg; Fibre 1.5g; Sodium 3mg.

Golden steamed sponge cake

Cakes are not traditionally served for dessert in China, but this light and tasty sponge is very popular and is often served on the dim sum trolley at lunchtime.

SERVES 8

175g/6oz/1½ cups plain
   (all-purpose) flour
5ml/1 tsp baking powder
1.5ml/¼ tsp bicarbonate of soda (baking
   soda)
3 large (US extra large) eggs
115g/4oz/²/₃ cup soft light
   brown sugar
45ml/3 tbsp walnut oil
30ml/2 tbsp golden
   (light corn) syrup
5ml/1 tsp vanilla extract

1 Sift the flour, baking powder and bicarbonate of soda into a large mixing bowl. Line an 18cm/7in diameter bamboo steamer or cake tin (pan) with baking parchment and set aside.

2 Whisk the eggs with the sugar until thick and frothy. Beat in the walnut oil and syrup, then set the mixture aside to rest for about 30 minutes.

3 Add the sifted flour, baking powder and bicarbonate of soda to the egg mixture with the vanilla extract, and beat rapidly to form a thick batter that is free from lumps.

4 Pour the batter into the steamer or pan. Cover and steam over boiling water for 30 minutes, until the sponge springs back when gently pressed with a finger. Leave to cool for a few minutes before serving.

Nutritional information per portion: Energy 150kcal/632kJ; Protein 4.4g; Carbohydrate 20g, of which sugars 3.3g; Fat 6.6g, of which saturates 1g; Cholesterol 71mg; Calcium 42mg; Fibre 0.7g; Sodium 37mg.

Water chestnut cake

Water chestnuts give a delightful texture to this Cantonese cake. The unusual sweet-savoury flavour makes it equally suitable for serving as a dessert or a snack.

SERVES 6

150g/5oz/1¼ cups water
    chestnut flour
200ml/7fl oz/scant 1 cup milk
200g/7oz can water
    chestnuts, drained
60ml/4 tbsp corn or vegetable oil
150g/5oz/¾ cup caster
    (superfine) sugar
400ml/14fl oz/1⅔ cups water

1 Put the water chestnut flour in a bowl and stir in the milk with a wooden spoon to make a smooth paste. Set aside.

2 In a food processor, grind the water chestnuts to a pulp. Add the oil, sugar and water and process until mixed.

3 Scrape the mixture into a pan and bring to the boil. Add half the water chestnut flour paste to the pan. Simmer, stirring, for 5 minutes.

4 Remove from the heat and leave to cool for 10 minutes. Add the remaining paste, a little at a time, stirring constantly. Return to the heat and cook, stirring, for 3 minutes, until as thick as double (heavy) cream.

5 Spoon into a pan which will fit in a steamer, then smooth the top. Steam for 30 minutes. Remove and leave to cool and set; it will be quite firm. Cut into squares and serve cold or fry lightly in oil to serve warm.

Nutritional information per portion: Energy 190kcal/800kJ; Protein 2.2g; Carbohydrate 29g, of which sugars 28.4g; Fat 8.1g, of which saturates 1.3g; Cholesterol 2mg; Calcium 60mg; Fibre 0.5g; Sodium 18mg.

Sesame and banana fritters

Small apple bananas, which have a lovely sweet flavour, are used here, but if you can't find them, you can use larger bananas instead – just cut into bitesize pieces.

SERVES 4

50g/2oz desiccated (dry unsweetened shredded) coconut
50g/2oz/¹/₄ cup golden caster (superfine) sugar
5ml/1 tsp ground cinnamon
2.5ml/¹/₂ tsp baking powder
115g/4oz/1 cup rice flour
30ml/2 tbsp sesame seeds
600ml/1 pint/2¹/₂ cups coconut milk
6 baby or apple bananas
sunflower oil, for deep-frying
icing (confectioners') sugar, to dust
vanilla ice cream, to serve

1 Place the coconut, golden caster sugar, cinnamon, baking powder, rice flour, sesame seeds and coconut milk in a large mixing bowl. Whisk thoroughly to form a smooth batter. Cover with clear film (plastic wrap) and chill for 30 minutes–1 hour.

2 Peel the bananas and carefully slice in half lengthways.

3 Fill a wok one-third full of sunflower oil and heat to 180°C/350°F (or until a cube of bread, dropped into the oil, browns in 40 seconds).

4 Working in batches, dip the halved bananas into the batter, drain off any excess and gently lower into the oil. Deep-fry for 3–4 minutes, or until golden.

5 Carefully remove the fried bananas from the wok using a slotted spoon and drain well on kitchen paper.

6 Dust the fritters liberally with icing sugar and serve them piping hot, with generous servings of vanilla ice cream.

Nutritional information per portion: Energy 204kcal/855kJ; Protein 3.9g; Carbohydrate 26.6g, of which sugars 14.8g; Fat 9.8g, of which saturates 4.4g; Cholesterol 48mg; Calcium 47mg; Fibre 1.7g; Sodium 75mg.

Chinese toffee apples

This classic dessert will make a great end to any meal. Wedges of apple are encased in a light batter, then dipped in crispy caramel to make a sweet, sticky dessert that is guaranteed to get stuck in your teeth! You can use baby bananas in place of the apples if you prefer.

SERVES 4

115g/4oz/1 cup plain
  (all-purpose) flour
10ml/2 tsp baking powder
60ml/4 tbsp cornflour (cornstarch)

4 firm eating apples
sunflower oil, for deep-frying
200g/7oz/1 cup caster
  (superfine) sugar

1 In a large mixing bowl, combine the flour, baking powder, cornflour and 175ml/6fl oz/³/₄ cup water. Stir to make a smooth batter and set aside.

2 Peel and core the apples, then cut each one into 8 thick wedges.

3 Fill a wok one-third full of oil and heat to 180°C/350°F (or until a cube of bread, dropped into the oil, browns in 40 seconds).

4 Working quickly, in batches, dip the apple wedges in the batter, drain off any excess and deep-fry for about 2 minutes, or until golden brown. Remove with a slotted spoon and drain on kitchen paper.

5 Reheat the oil to 180°C/350°F and re-fry the apple wedges again for 2 minutes. Drain well on kitchen paper and set aside.

6 Very carefully, pour off all but 30ml/2 tbsp of the oil from the wok and stir in the sugar. Heat gently until the sugar melts and starts to caramelize. When the mixture is light brown, add a few pieces of apple at a time and toss to coat evenly.

7 Fill a large bowl with ice cubes and chilled water. Plunge the coated apple pieces briefly into the iced water to harden the caramel, then remove with a slotted spoon and serve immediately.

Nutritional information per portion: Energy 457kcal/1940kJ; Protein 3.4g; Carbohydrate 97.3g, of which sugars 61.6g; Fat 8.8g, of which saturates 1.1g; Cholesterol 0mg; Calcium 73mg; Fibre 2.5g; Sodium 14mg.

Sweet and spicy rice fritters

These delicious little golden balls of rice are scented with sweet, warm spices and will fill the kitchen with wonderful aromas while you're cooking. Serve dusted with sugar and piping hot.

SERVES 4

175g/6oz cooked basmati rice
2 eggs, lightly beaten
60ml/4 tbsp caster (superfine) sugar
a pinch of freshly grated nutmeg
2.5ml/¹/₂ tsp ground cinnamon
a pinch of ground cloves
10ml/2 tsp vanilla extract
50g/2oz/¹/₂ cup plain
    (all-purpose) flour
10ml/2 tsp baking powder
a pinch of salt
25g/1oz desiccated (dry unsweetened
    shredded) coconut
sunflower oil, for deep-frying
icing (confectioners') sugar,
    to dust

1 Place the cooked rice, eggs, sugar, nutmeg, cinnamon, cloves and vanilla extract in a large bowl and whisk to combine. Sift in the flour, baking powder and salt and add the coconut. Mix well until thoroughly combined.

2 Fill a wok one-third full of the oil and heat to 180°C/350°F (or until a cube of bread, dropped into the oil, browns in 40 seconds).

3 Very gently, drop tablespoonfuls of the mixture into the oil, one at a time, and fry for 2–3 minutes, or until golden. Carefully remove the fritters from the wok using a slotted spoon and drain well on kitchen paper.

4 Divide the fritters into four portions, or simply pile them up on a single large platter. Dust them with icing sugar and serve immediately.

Nutritional information per portion: Energy 316kcal/1321kJ; Protein 6.6g; Carbohydrate 45.7g, of which sugars 16.3g; Fat 12.4g, of which saturates 4.8g; Cholesterol 95mg; Calcium 46mg; Fibre 1.3g; Sodium 38mg.

Crispy mango wontons with raspberry sauce

These crisp, golden parcels are perfect for a casual supper. The sweet raspberry sauce looks stunning drizzled over the wontons and tastes even better.

SERVES 4

2 firm, ripe mangoes
24 fresh wonton wrappers
(approximately 7.5cm/3in square)
vegetable oil, for deep-frying
icing (confectioners') sugar, to dust

FOR THE SAUCE

400g/14oz/3½ cups raspberries
45ml/3 tbsp icing
(confectioners') sugar
a squeeze of lemon juice

1 Place the raspberries and icing sugar in a food processor and blend until smooth. Press the raspberry purée through a sieve (strainer) to remove the seeds, then stir a squeeze of lemon juice into the sauce. Chill until ready to serve.

2 Peel each mango, then carefully slice the flesh away from one side of the flat stone (pit). Repeat on the second side, then trim off any remaining flesh from around the stone. Cut the mango flesh into 1cm/½in dice.

3 Lay 12 wonton wrappers on a clean work surface and place 10ml/2 tsp of the chopped mangoes in the centre of each one. Brush the edges with water and top with the remaining wonton wrappers. Press the edges to seal.

4 Heat the oil in a wok to 180°C/350°F (or until a cube of bread, dropped into the oil, browns in 40 seconds). Deep-fry the wontons, 2–3 at a time, for about 2 minutes, or until golden. Remove from the oil and drain on kitchen paper. Dust with icing sugar and serve with the raspberry sauce.

Nutritional information per portion: Energy 314kcal/1331kJ; Protein 5.5g; Carbohydrate 56.1g, of which sugars 27.3g; Fat 9.2g, of which saturates 1.2g; Cholesterol 0mg; Calcium 93mg; Fibre 5.6g; Sodium 6mg.

Egg tarts

These delectable little tarts demonstrate the hybrid Portuguese-Chinese nature of the food from Macau, which was a Portuguese enclave for over four hundred years. Over the centuries, these have become a favourite throughout the region and are the only Chinese dessert containing cheese.

MAKES 24

150ml/¹/₄ pint/²/₃ cup single (light) cream
   or whipping cream
75ml/5 tbsp sugar
45g/1¹/₂oz mild Cheddar cheese, grated
3 large eggs (US extra large), lightly beaten

a pinch of salt
2.5ml/¹/₂ tsp vanilla extract
175ml/6fl oz/³/₄ cup full cream (whole) milk
450g/1lb shortcrust pastry,
   thawed if frozen

1 Pour the cream into a large, heavy pan and stir in the sugar. Heat gently, stirring continuously, until the sugar dissolves, then bring to the boil, still stirring. Be careful not to let the mixture stick on the bottom or it will burn.

2 Add the cheese to the cream mixture and cook over a low heat until the cheese melts and the mixture is smooth. Remove the pan from the heat and set aside until the mixture has cooled a little.

3 In a bowl, beat the eggs lightly with the salt. Add to the cream mixture with the vanilla extract and milk. Strain through a fine sieve (strainer) into a clean bowl.

4 Preheat the oven to 200°C/400°F/Gas 6. On a lightly floured surface, roll out the pastry to a thickness of around 3mm/¹/₈in, and cut out 24 rounds with a pastry cutter. Fit these into two 12-hole tartlet tins (muffin pans), pressing them down gently.

5 Pour the filling into the pastry cases, filling them almost to the top. Bake for 20 minutes or until the filling has set and is golden brown. Remove from the tins and cool on wire racks. Serve warm.

Nutritional information per portion: Energy 131kcal/549kJ; Protein 3g; Carbohydrate 12.5g, of which sugars 3.9g; Fat 8g, of which saturates 3.1g; Cholesterol 37mg; Calcium 50mg; Fibre 0.4g; Sodium 104mg.

The Chinese kitchen

Creating authentic Chinese meals is

easily achieved with a small selection

of specialist tools and a fragrant larder

of deliciously-fresh ingredients.

This final chapter looks at the key

components of the Chinese kitchen,

from woks, bamboo steamers and clay

pots, through to the plethora of unique

ingredients and flavourings that are

integral to the cuisine.

Equipment and utensils

The equipment in the average Western kitchen will be perfectly adequate for most of the recipes in this book, particularly now that the wok has become indispensable in many households. There are items, however, that will make cooking Chinese food easier and more pleasurable. The fact that many of these simple pieces of equipment also look good, and instantly establish you as an adventurous cook in the eyes of your friends is a bonus.

Cleaver

A cleaver can seem intimidating, but in reality cleavers are very useful. The blade of a heavy cleaver is powerful enough to cut through bone, yet delicate enough in the hands of a master chef to create paper thin slices of raw fish. The flat of the broad blade is ideal for crushing garlic, and the same blade can be used to convey the crushed items to the wok or pan.

ABOVE:
A traditional Chinese Grater

Grater

Traditional graters, used for preparing ginger, galangal and mooli (daikon), are made from wood or bamboo, but a metal cheese grater makes a satisfactory substitute.

Mortar and pestle

Oriental cooks prefer granite or stone mortars and pestles, since these have rough surfaces which help to grip the ingredients that are being ground or pounded. Bigger, flat-bowled mortars are good for making spice pastes that contain large amounts of fresh spices, onion, herbs and garlic.

ABOVE:
A stone mortar and pestle.

Spice mill

If you are going to grind a lot of spices, a spice mill will prove useful. An electric coffee grinder works well for this purpose, but it is a good idea to reserve the mill for spices, unless you like to have your coffee flavoured with cardamom or cloves.

Wok

It is not surprising that the wok has become a universal favourite, for it is a remarkably versatile utensil.

BELOW: *A steel wok.*

The rounded bottom was originally designed to fit snugly on a traditional Chinese brazier or stove. It conducts and retains heat evenly and because of its shape, the food always returns to the centre where the heat is most intense. This makes it ideally suited for stir-frying, braising, steaming, boiling and even for deep-frying.

Although the wok might not at first glance appear to be the best utensil for deep-frying, it is actually ideal, requiring far less oil than a flat-bottomed deep-fryer. The narrow base of the wok allows oil to pool, meaning that food can be deep-fried in minimal amounts of oil.

A new carbonized steel wok must be seasoned before use. The best way to do this is to place the wok over a high heat until the surface blackens, then wash it in warm, soapy water. Use a stiff brush to get the wok clean, then rinse it well in clean water and place it over a medium heat to dry completely. Finally, wipe the surface with a pad of kitchen paper soaked in vegetable oil. After each use, wash the wok under the hot water tap, but never use detergent as this would remove the "seasoning" and cause the wok to rust.

ABOVE:
*A selection
of wok tools.*

Wok tools

Some wok sets come with a spatula and ladle made from cast iron or stainless steel. These are very useful, particularly the ladle. In addition to its obvious purpose as a stirrer, it can be used to measure small quantities of liquid. A standard ladle holds about 175ml/6fl oz/$^3/_4$cup of liquid. A dome-shaped lid is also useful, as is a metal draining rack that fits over the wok. Small items such as deep-fried foods can be placed on the rack to keep warm while successive batches are cooked.

Strainers

Several types of strainer are available, but the two most useful are the perforated metal scoop or slotted spoon, and the coarse-mesh, wire skimmer, preferably with a long bamboo handle. Wire skimmers come in a variety of sizes and are useful for removing food from hot oil when deep-frying.

Steamers

The traditional Chinese steamer is made from bamboo and has a tight-fitting lid. Several sizes are available, and you can stack as many tiers as you like over a wok of boiling water. The modern steamer is free-standing and made of aluminium, but the food cooked in a metal steamer lacks the subtle fragrance that a bamboo steamer imparts. There are also electric steamers available – which work in much the same way as bamboo and aluminium steamers, but are self-contained and do not need to be placed on the hob. The bamboo variety has the biggest impact at a traditional Chinese banquet.

ABOVE: *An authentic bamboo steamer.*

Clay pot

Also known as the sand-pot or Chinese casserole, this earthenware cooking utensil must have preceded the cast-iron pot by thousands of years. Several shapes and sizes are available, and most are glazed on the inside only. They are not expensive and can be bought in Asian or Chinese stores. With care, the pots can be used on top of the stove, where they retain an even heat.

ABOVE: *A traditional clay pot.*

Mongolian firepot

Also known as a Chinese hotpot, this is not unlike a fondue pot, in that it allows food to be cooked at the table. The design is different from that of a fondue pot, however, as it consists of a central funnel, which is filled with burning charcoal, surrounded by a moat in which hot stock is placed. The pot is placed in the centre of the table and guests cook small pieces of meat and vegetables in the hot stock. Once these are all cooked and eaten, the stock is served as a soup. There are several different models available, the most expensive being made of brass, while the cheaper ones are made of aluminium or stainless steel.

Poultry

Chicken and duck are popular the world over, and nowhere is this more amply illustrated than in China, where they are used in soups, salads, stir-fries, curries, roasts and braised dishes. Every part of the bird is utilized, including the liver, gizzard, heart and even the feet.

ABOVE: *A chicken carcass.*

CHICKEN

The chicken is a descendant of a South-east Asian jungle fowl that was domesticated over 4,500 years ago. Today chicken features in almost every cuisine. Its universal popularity is due to the fact that the flesh combines happily with a huge variety of different ingredients.

•Preparation and cooking techniques

Chicken can be cooked whole, jointed, or taken off the bone and chopped or cut into thin strips – this is the usual practice if the meat is to be stir-fried. In China, chicken breasts on the bone are sometimes cut into as many as 20 pieces before being stir-fried, and the ability of the Chinese to pick up these tiny pieces with chopsticks and to remove the meat from the bone in the mouth is a marvel of dexterity.

Serving meats and other foods in manageable morsels is the norm in China, where knives are viewed as weapons, and therefore inappropriate for meals. Chopsticks are acceptable, as they are seen as harmless.

Throughout the East, frugality is a virtue, so one chicken might be used in three dishes: the breasts sliced in strips for a stir-fry; the rest of the meat braised in a red cooked dish or a curry; and the carcass utilized for stock.

The skill that is exhibited by Chinese cooks with the simplest equipment is testament to their creative love of food. Using a cleaver and a small sharp knife, a chicken can be chopped into appropriate portions in no time at all.

DUCK

A symbol of happiness and fidelity, duck is a very popular ingredient in Chinese cuisine. Duck is central to celebratory meals, and is served in countless imaginative ways. At Chinese New Year, for instance, duck is an essential part of every banquet.

BELOW: *A duck carcass.*

•Preparation and cooking techniques

The most famous duck dish has to be Peking duck. The classic way of making this universally popular restaurant dish involves hanging the prepared birds in a windy place to dry before roasting them in a special oven. At one time only the skin was eaten, but it is now more usual to eat the succulent meat as well. This is wrapped in a Mandarin pancake which has been spread with a little plum sauce and sprinkled with a few pieces of shredded spring onion (scallion) and slivers of cucumber. This dish is so popular that it is now possible to buy ready-made portions of Peking duck, with all the trimmings, in the West.

The Chinese technique for preparing duck for roasting involves pricking the skin lightly all over with a fork, placing the bird on a trivet in the sink, then pouring a kettle of freshly boiled water over the top. The bird is then drained well, and the cavity wiped with kitchen paper, before being suspended from duck hooks or butcher's hooks and left to dry overnight. Once the bird is dry, the skin is sprinkled with a little salt. The bird is then placed on a trivet in a roasting pan and roasted in a hot oven until the skin is quite crisp and golden brown and the bird is fully cooked.

If the duck is to be jointed for use in a curry or stir-fry then the same procedure can be used as for chicken.

Meat

Pork is the most popular meat in Chinese cuisine, and is used in a wide range of traditional dishes. Beef and mutton are less common, but are used in parts of the country with large Muslim communites, where the use of pork is prohibited.

PORK

This is as popular as chicken in China. Like chicken, it blends happily with a wide range of ingredients, from vegetables to shellfish, and is equally at home with salted and pickled foods.

Wherever there are Muslim communities, however, pork is off limits and either beef or lamb is served instead. This is especially true in north-western China, where there are many Muslim Hui people.

ABOVE: *Various cuts of pork.*

• Preparation and cooking techniques

For stir-frying, fillet, lean leg or belly are the preferred cuts, along with the meaty parts of chops or spare ribs. The meat is cut into thin shreds so that it responds to really quick cooking over high heat, which is economical in the use of fuel. For casseroles and braised dishes shoulder, spare ribs or belly pork might be used, and the meat is often cooked for so long that it forms a luscious jelly-like mixture.

Chinese Sausages

Although these are described as Chinese sausages, they are made throughout South-east Asia and are widely available in the West. There are two types: a pink and white sausage, which is made from pork and pork fat, and a darker sausage, in which the pork is mixed with duck liver.

The sausages are about 15cm/6in long and about 2cm/^{3}/$_4$in thick, and are sold in pairs. The dried sausages do not have any aroma, but as soon as they are cooked they become fragrant and sweet. The best way of cooking them is to cut them diagonally into thin slices, then steam them on top of the rice for 10 minutes or so. Alternatively, the sausage can be steamed for 10 minutes, then skinned and sliced before adding to dishes such as fried rice. They will keep for several months in the refrigerator.

ABOVE: *Chinese sausages.*

BEEF AND LAMB

The use of beef in Chinese cuisine is relatively recent, because cattle were considered beasts of burden and highly valued as such. The buffalo, too, has always been used widely, mainly in the paddy fields to plough the land prior to planting by hand.

Beef and lamb are traditionally eaten only in the north of China and where there are Muslim communities. However, because of the proximity of Beijing to the northern provinces and the number of Chinese Muslim restaurants in the capital, lamb and beef are becoming increasingly popular there, too.

Lamb is cooked in the famous Mongolian firepot, while beef is used in many different types of recipes, mainly as a substitute for pork. It is generally thinly sliced and used for dishes where a quick method of cooking such as stir-frying is required.

Fish and shellfish

Fish is an extremely important source of protein throughout China, whose coastal waters, rivers and lakes provide an abundant harvest.

COD

This is closely related to, and interchangeable with, many other related species of white-fleshed fish such as haddock, hake, ling and whiting. Cod holds its texture well and can be cooked in many different ways, but it is important not to overcook it.

GREY MULLET

Varieties of grey mullet are found all over the world. The beautiful silvery fish resemble sea bass, but have larger scales and small mouths. A good grey mullet has lean, slightly soft, creamy white flesh with a pleasant flavour.

PLAICE

These fish have smooth, dark greyish-brown skin with orange spots and the underside is pearly white. They have soft, rather bland white flesh, which can sometimes lack flavour.

SOLE

Arguably the finest fish of all. Dover have a firm, delicate flesh with a superb flavour. Sole are best three days after they are caught, so if you are sure that you are buying fish straight from the sea, keep them a couple of days before cooking. The skin should be sticky and the underside very white.

ABOVE: *Cod fillets.*

EELS

There are more than 20 members of the eel family. All are snake-like fish with smooth slippery skin and spineless fins. Eels are a popular food throughout Asia. They should be bought alive, as they go off very quickly once dead. Ask the fishmonger to kill and skin them and to chop them up into 5cm/2in lengths.

SALMON

The finest wild salmon has a superb flavour and is a healthy choice being full of Omega-3 fatty acids. It is a costly fish, however, and so it may not be affordable on a regular basis. Responsibly farmed salmon is more economical, and it is still delicious. The rosy flesh is beautifully moist and responds very well to being poached

ABOVE: *Plaice.*

or baked, either on its own or with herbs and spices or aromatics. When buying fresh salmon, have a good fishmonger cut you a chunk from a large salmon for the best results; do not use ready-cut steaks.

SEA TROUT

They closely resemble salmon, but have smaller less pointed heads and squarer tails. They have fine, dark pink flesh, which is beautifully succulent and has a delicate, mellow flavour.

SEA BASS

Characterized by the delicate flavour of its flesh, sea bass is enjoyed throughout Asia. It holds its shape when cooked, and can be grilled (broiled), steamed, baked or cooked on a barbecue whole. Sea bass fillets taste delicious when they have been marinated, then cooked on a ridged griddle pan. Chunks or strips make a sensational stir-fry.

GROUPER

These are members of the extensive sea bass family. They look extremely gloomy, with upturned protruding lips. Groupers are available all year round, and can be cooked in the same ways as sea bass.

SNAPPER

There are more than 250 species of snapper throughout the world. The best-known is the red snapper, which is bright red all over. Snapper is a versatile fish that can be baked, poached, pan-fried, grilled (broiled) and steamed.

ABOVE: *A blue crab.*

MONKFISH

The monkfish tail is one of the finest cuts of all fish, with a superb firm texture and a delicious sweetness, rather like lobster meat. Monkfish is available all year, but is best in spring and summer before spawning. It is sold as whole tails, fillets or medallions.

CARP

This freshwater fish is widely farmed in Asia. It has meaty, moist flesh with a distinctive taste. When buying carp, ask the fishmonger to remove the scales and strong dorsal fins.

A favourite way of cooking carp is to stuff it with ginger and spring onions (scallions) and serve it with a sweet pickle sauce.

ABOVE: *Scallops.*

TUNA

This very large fish is usually sold as steaks. The flesh should be solid and compact. Tuna loses its colour and can become dry when overcooked, so cook it briefly over high heat, or stew it gently with moist ingredients like tomatoes and peppers.

SQUID

Squid is an ideal candidate for stir-frying with flavours like ginger, garlic, spring onion (scallion) and chilli, and it will also make an interesting salad. For a slow-cooked dish, try squid cooked in a clay pot with chillies and noodles.

LOBSTER

This luxury shellfish is usually served as a restaurant dish. To cook a live lobster, put it in a pan of ice-cold water, cover the pan tightly and bring the water to the boil. The shell will turn bright red and the flesh will be tender and succulent when the lobster is cooked.

CRAB

Tender crab meat has a distinctive taste that goes well with Chinese flavours. A popular variety are the soft-shell crabs which are blue crabs that have shed their hard carapaces, leaving them deliciously soft, with sweet creamy flesh.

SCALLOPS

The tender, sweet flesh of this shellfish needs very little cooking. Whenever possible, buy scallops fresh. In cooked dishes, the coral can be retained and is regarded as a delicacy.

ABOVE: *Tuna steaks.*

MUSSELS

This shellfish is widely used in Chinese cooking. Farmed mussels are now readily available and they are usually relatively free of barnacles. Discard any that are not closed, or which fail to shut when tapped. The best way to cook mussels is to steam them in a small amount of flavoured liquor in a large pan for 3–4 minutes until the shells open.

SHRIMPS AND PRAWNS

If you ask for shrimp in Britain, then you will be given tiny crustaceans, while in the United States, the term is used to describe the larger shellfish which the British refer to as prawns. However, Chinese cooks use both words fairly indiscriminately, so check what a recipe requires. Buy raw shellfish whenever possible, and then cook it yourself.

Dried shrimps are especially popular in China. They are pale pink in colour, having been boiled before being spread out in the sun to dry. Dried shrimps have a very strong smell, and the flavour is sharp and salty. Because of their strong taste, they are usually used as seasoning rather than an independent ingredient, and are often used in rice dishes and to garnish salads.

Vegetables

In China cooks use vegetables freely in stir-fries and braised dishes, and have evolved a wide range of delicious vegetarian main courses to make the most of the abundant choice of vegetables on sale in markets. Many of these vegetables are now commonplace in other parts of the world. Chinese leaves (Chinese cabbage), pak choi (bok choy) and beansprouts are usually available in supermarkets, and other greens, such as mizuna, Chinese mustard greens and Chinese broccoli (kai lan), are often grown by small producers and can be found at farmers' markets.

CHINESE LEAVES

Also known as Chinese cabbage or Napa cabbage, this vegetable has pale green, crinkly leaves with long, wide, white ribs. It is pleasantly crunchy, has a sweet, nutty flavour and tastes wonderful raw or cooked. When buying Chinese leaves, look out for firm, slightly heavy heads with pale green leaves without blemishes or bruises.

BELOW:
Choi sum.

ABOVE: *Pak choi (bok choy).*

PAK CHOI (BOK CHOY)

Another member of the brassica family, pak choi (bok choy) has lots of noms-de-plume, including horse's ear and Chinese white cabbage. Unlike Chinese leaves, pak choi doesn't keep well, so plan to use it within a day or two of purchase. The vegetable is generally cooked, although very young and tender pak choi can be eaten raw. The stems – regarded by many as the best part – need slightly longer cooking than the leaves.

CHOI SUM

Often sold in bunches, choi sum has bright green leaves and thin, pale, slightly grooved stems. It has a pleasant aroma and mild taste, and remains crisp and tender if properly cooked. The leaves can be sliced, but are more often steamed whole. Choi sum will keep for a few days in the salad drawer, but is best used as soon as possible after purchase.

CHINESE BROCCOLI

Also known as kai lan, this has a somewhat straggly appearance, and looks more like purple sprouting broccoli than tight Calabrese. Every part of Chinese broccoli is edible, and each has its own inimitable taste. To prepare, remove the tough outer leaves, then cut off the leaves. If the stems are tough, peel them. It is usual to blanch the vegetable briefly in salted boiling water or stock before stir-frying.

ABOVE:
Chinese broccoli.

AUBERGINES (EGGPLANTS)

Popular throughout China, aubergines come in a variety of shapes, sizes and colours. They have a smoky, slightly bitter taste and spongy flesh that readily absorbs other flavours and oils. To avoid the absorption of too much fat, cut the aubergine into slices, and dry-fry these in a wok over medium heat for 4–5 minutes. They can also be braised, stuffed or baked.

ABOVE:
Aubergine.

ABOVE: *Mooli.*

MOOLI (DAIKON)

This Asian vegetable looks rather like a parsnip, but is actually related to the radish. The flavour is milder than that of most radishes, however, although the texture is similar: crisp and crunchy. Treat it like a carrot, scraping or peeling the outer skin and then slicing it in rounds or batons. It can be eaten raw or cooked.

POTATOES AND SWEET POTATOES

Although potatoes and sweet potatoes are unrelated, this was not appreciated when they first reached Asia, and they were both given the same Chinese name. In northern China white potatoes are a staple food, although not as important as noodles; in southern China they are far less significant.

YAMS

Yams are believed to have originated in China, but are now grown in all tropical regions. The Chinese yam has fine whiskers and the flesh is creamy white.

TARO

This root vegetable requires warm, damp growing conditions and is usually harvested in the winter. Generally, it comes in two varieties. One is small and egg-shaped; the other is about 25cm/10in long and shaped like a barrel. Both are covered in short hairs with white purple-flecked flesh. Taro is used like a potato – mashed and baked, or added to soups, stews and curries. The larger variety is firm with a nutty flavour; the smaller one is creamier and sweeter, lending itself to sweet cakes and puddings.

LUFFA SQUASH

Dark green with ridges running lengthways, luffa squash has sweet and spongy flesh and is usually harvested when it is about 30cm/1ft long. Generally, it is sliced and used in stir-fries and soups, much the same way as you would cook a courgette (zucchini). Luffa squash is available in Asian markets.

Keep fresh luffa in the refrigerator, but do not store it for too long as within 2–3 days of purchase it will start to go limp.

ABOVE: *Yam.*

KABOCHA SQUASH

This is a stout, pumpkin-shaped vegetable with a beautiful dark-green skin patterned with yellow spots and green lines. The flesh is pale orange, fragrant, sweet and creamy, lending itself to a variety of dishes, including curries and desserts. An average kabocha weighs about 1–1.5kg/2–3lb and has edible skin. They are readily available in specialist Asian markets and some supermarkets.

BELOW: *Luffa squash.*

LEFT: *Sweet potatoes.*

ABOVE: *Winter melon.*

WINTER MELON

Large, mild-flavoured gourds, winter melons can weigh 5.4kg/12lb or more and grow up to 25cm/10in in diameter. Egg- or pear-shaped and dark green, they are harvested in the summer (but traditionally stored for winter) and sold whole or cut into wedges. The white flesh tastes like marrow or courgette (zucchini) and is believed to cool fevers. Prepared and cooked in the same way as a pumpkin, winter melon is added to soups, stews and stir-fries, as the flesh absorbs the flavours of the dish. The

BELOW: *Fresh bamboo shoots.*

rind must be cut off and the seeds and coarse fibres at the centre scooped out before the flesh is cut into strips or wedges. Winter melons and fuzzy melons can be used interchangeably, as they are similar in flavour. Both come in various shapes and sizes and are available in Asian markets and supermarkets.

BAMBOO SHOOTS

Fresh bamboo shoots are quite hard to buy outside Asia, but you may find them in big-city Asian markets. They must be parboiled before being cooked, as the raw vegetable contains a highly toxic oil. Remove the base and the hard outer leaves, then cut the core into chunks. Boil these in salted water for 30 minutes, then drain, rinse under cold water and drain again. Cut into slices, shreds or cubes for further cooking. Dried bamboo slices must be soaked in water for 2–3 hours before use. Canned bamboo shoots only need rinsing before being used.

WATER CHESTNUTS

Fresh, crisp water chestnuts are the corms of a plant that grows on the margins of rivers and lakes. Their snow-white flesh stays crunchy even after long cooking. Fresh water chestnuts are often available from Asian markets. They keep well in a paper

ABOVE: *Water chestnuts.*

bag in the refrigerator. Once released from their dark brown jackets, they must be kept submerged in water in a covered container and used within one week. Canned water chestnuts should be rinsed before being used.

BEANSPROUTS

Mung beans and soya beans are the varieties of beansprout most often used, and they are an important ingredient in the Chinese kitchen. They should be used as fresh as possible. If you can, sprout the beans yourself. Before use, rinse them to remove the husks and tiny roots. Use them in salads or stir-fries, but take care not to overcook them, or they will become limp and tasteless.

ONIONS

The common onion so widely used in the West is known as "foreign onion" in Asia, where shallots and spring onions (scallions) are generally preferred. They come in a wide variety of sizes and colours from huge

ABOVE: *An onion.*

golden-skinned globes to smaller, milder red and white onions. It is a very versatile vegetable. It can be eaten fried, boiled, steamed or raw, and it is an essential component of a great number of sauces, and dishes such as curries and stews. There is no mistaking the strong aroma and flavour of the onion. It is used as a flavouring ingredient throughout China, but is seldom served on its own as a side vegetable. Fried onions are a popular garnish, especially in South-east Asia.

SPRING ONIONS (SCALLIONS)

Slender and crisp, spring onions (scallions) are appreciated by Chinese cooks

ABOVE: *Spring onions.*

not only for their aroma and flavour, but also for their perceived cooling qualities. Use spring onions raw in salads or lightly cooked in stir-fries. They need very little preparation. Just trim off the roots, strip off the wilted outer leaves and separate the white and green parts.

SHALLOTS

Although they belong to the same family as garlic, leeks, chives and onions – and look suspiciously like baby onions – shallots are very much their own vegetable. Sometimes called bunching onions, they have bulbs that multiply to produce clusters joined at the root end. Shallots tend to be sweeter and much milder than large onions. Indispensable in Chinese kitchens, shallots are far more popular than both regular onions and spring onions (scallions) for everyday use.

CHINESE CHIVES

Although they belong to the same family, Chinese chives are quite different from the Western variety, both in their appearance and taste. Two species are available: one has long, flat green leaves like a small, thin leek, the other has long, tubular stalks with a single bud at the tip. Chinese chives have a much stronger aroma than the ones

ABOVE: *Chinese chives.*

grown in the West. They don't really taste of onions, but have a flavour that resembles a cross between garlic and leek. They are either served as a vegetable in their own right, or used as an ingredient in cooked dishes. A popular Chinese vegetarian dish features chopped chives cooked with scrambled eggs and tofu. Chinese chives are always sold as leaves only, without the bulb. Uniformly dark green leaves are good, and any that are turning yellow should be discarded. Wash well, drain, then chop or slice into short sections. Cantonese cooks often blanch chives in boiling water or stock for a minute or two before stir-frying.

BELOW: *Shallots.*

Fresh and dried mushrooms

Mushrooms are ubiquitous in Chinese cuisine. Many varieties are used, including shiitake, cloud ear (wood ear), enoki, oyster, silver ear and cloud mushrooms. They are often dried and then reconstituted in water before being added to stews, soups and stir-fries.

SHIITAKE

Fresh shiitake mushrooms used to be a rarity in the West, but are now cultivated and are freely available in supermarkets. They resemble large, brown button mushrooms in appearance, and they grow on hardwood logs. Although small mushrooms can be eaten raw, cooking brings out their flavour. They are used in soups, stir-fries and braised dishes. They are a popular ingredient in vegetarian dishes, and go well with noodles and rice. They have a slightly acidic taste and contain twice as much protein as button mushrooms.

BELOW: *Oyster mushrooms.*

Their flavour is intensified when they are dried. They are good combined with less strongly flavoured food.

OYSTER MUSHROOMS

In the wild, oyster mushrooms grow in clumps on rotting wood. The caps, gills and stems are all the same colour, which can be pearl grey, pink or yellow. Once thought of exclusively as wild mushrooms, they are now grown commercially and are widely available in Western supermarkets. Their aroma is fairly mild, with a slight suggestion of seafood. They are popular in soups and stir-fries, and they are also used in noodle and rice dishes.

Buy oyster mushrooms that smell and look fresh, avoiding any with damp, slimy patches and those that have discoloured. Store in a paper bag in the vegetable compartment of the refrigerator, and use as soon as possible after purchase. They do not keep for more than 2–3 days.

ENOKI MUSHROOMS

Also called enokitake, these are slender and exceedingly delicate mushrooms with long thin stems and tiny white caps. The Chinese name – "golden needle mushrooms" – is the same as that given to the dried tiger lily buds which they resemble.

Enoki mushrooms have a delicate, sweet and almost fruity flavour, and a deliciously crisp

ABOVE: *Enoki mushrooms.*

texture that is best appreciated if they are added raw to salads or lightly cooked and used as a garnish for soups or hot dishes.

If bought fresh, enoki mushrooms will keep for 4–5 days in the salad compartment of a refrigerator. Avoid any that have damp, slimy patches.

STRAW MUSHROOMS

These small, grey-brown mushrooms are grown on beds of rice straw, hence the name. A native to China, they were introduced to the rest of South-

BELOW: *Canned straw mushrooms.*

east Asia by Chinese immigrants. Fresh straw mushrooms are not readily available in the West, but dried ones can sometimes be found in Asian or Chinese stores. Straw mushrooms have an even stronger aroma than Chinese dried black mushrooms. Canned straw mushrooms are widely available in Asian stores; they have a delicate, silky surface with a subtle, sweet taste and an unusual slippery texture. Beacuse they have an almost neutral flavour, straw mushrooms can be combined with all sorts of ingredients in stir fries, braised dishes and soups. They are an essential ingredient in many Chinese dishes, and they are also used for making mushroom soy sauce.

DRIED BLACK MUSHROOMS/ FRAGRANT MUSHROOMS

Dried black mushrooms are widely used throughout Asia, and are exported around the world. Although they are frequently labelled as "Chinese", to distinguish them from other dried mushrooms, and have come to be widely known as such, the majority of dried black mushrooms sold in Asian stores actually come

ABOVE: *Cloud ear mushrooms.*

from Japan, which produces more dried black mushrooms than does China. There are generally three different grades of dried black mushrooms, with caps that range in colour from dark grey, to brown-black or tan. The cheapest of these has quite thin caps, may be sold with or without stalks, and may well be labelled "fragrant mushrooms", which is the generic term for shiitake mushrooms. Next come the "winter mushrooms" which have thicker caps and a more fleshy texture. The most expensive type are called "flower mushrooms". These are the best of the winter mushrooms. The caps are so thick that they crack, revealing the flower pattern that earned them their name. All three have a dusky aroma with a fragrant flavour, which is much intensified by the drying process.

CLOUD EARS (WOOD EARS)

Also known as tree mushrooms or simply dried black fungus, these are widely used in China. The dried fungi are thin and brittle, and look like pieces of charred paper. There is a slightly smoky smell when cloud ears are first removed from the packet, but this disappears once they have been soaked. They are almost tasteless, but have an intriguing texture, which is slippery yet crisp.

SILVER EARS

Also known as dried white fungus, this earned its Chinese name of "silver ear" partly because of its rarity, and partly because of the high price it

ABOVE: *Silver ear mushrooms.*

fetches on account of its medicinal value. It is regarded as being an excellent tonic, and is also used for the relief of insomnia and lung and liver diseases. Silver ears do not belong to the same genus as cloud ears. Although the texture is similar, white fungus has a sweeter flavour.

BELOW. *A selection of dried Chinese mushrooms, including cloud ear, silver ear and dried black mushrooms.*

Fruit and nuts

Many fruits grown in China are eaten as snacks or palate cleansers, especially following strong flavoured, spicy meals. Nuts are also eaten as snacks, often as an accompaniment to tea, or used to garnish savoury dishes.

LYCHEES
The pearly white flesh of these moist little fruits can be nibbled off the stone (pit), or sliced and used in a fruit salad or savoury dish. Chinese cooks like to pair lychees with pork. They also go well with clementines. When buying fresh lychees, choose ones with pink or red shells; brown fruit are past their prime.

MANGOES
There are many types of mango. Most are oval in shape with blushed gold or pink skin, although there are also green, scarlet and orange varieties. All are highly scented, with meltingly soft flesh that is invariably sweet and juicy. When buying mangoes, choose fruit with smooth, unblemished skin.

ABOVE: *Lychees.*

ABOVE: *Asian pears.*

If mango chunks are required for a recipe, the easiest way to obtain these is to cut a thick lengthways slice off either side of the unpeeled fruit. Score the flesh on each slice with criss-cross lines, cutting down to the skin. Fold these slices inside out and then slice off the flesh, which will be neatly cubed.

KUMQUATS
Although these look like tiny citrus fruits, they belong to a species of fruit classified as fortunella. About the size of a large olive, the fruits have thin orange-coloured edible rind. This is sweet and provides an interesting contrast to the tangy pulp it encloses. Kumquats can be eaten whole, halved or sliced into rings.

ASIAN PEARS
Asian pears do not soften when ripe, and are valued for their crunch. There are several varieties, most of which are round, rather than the conventional pear-shape, with golden or russet skin.

STAR FRUIT (CARAMBOLA)
Cylindrical in shape, this bright yellow fruit has five "wings" which form the points of the star shapes. Fresh fruits are sweet, but those that have travelled long distances can be disappointing.

CASHEW NUTS
These popular nuts have a sweet flavour and crumbly texture. They are never sold in the shell, since removing the seed from its outer casing requires an extensive heating process.

CANDLENUTS
These look rather like macadamia nuts and are used as a thickener in Asian cooking. They are slightly toxic when raw, so must always be cooked.

CHINESE CHESTNUTS
These are sweeter than the Western variety. They have a meaty texture and robust flavour, and taste particularly good with Chinese leaves (Chinese cabbage).

SESAME SEEDS
These tiny seeds are flat and pear-shaped. Raw seeds have little aroma and are almost tasteless until they are roasted or dry-fried, which brings out their nutty flavour and aroma.

LOTUS SEEDS
Fresh lotus seeds are used as a snack food. The dried seeds must be soaked in water before use. The seeds are prized for their texture and ability to absorb other flavours. They are often added to soups.

ABOVE: *Star fruit.*

Flavourings and sauces

The principal flavourings favoured in China have made a tremendous contribution to global cuisine. Ingredients like fresh ginger and lime now feature on menus the world over, not just in recipes that reflect their origin, but also in fusion food. Soy sauce is now a commonplace condiment and is often used in dishes that have no more than a nodding acquaintance with China.

GARLIC

Often used with spring onions (scallions) and ginger, garlic is an important ingredient in China. The most common variety in East Asia has a purple skin, a fairly distinctive aroma and a hint of sweetness. In Taiwan, immature green garlic is popular. Garlic may dominate a dish, but is also used in more subtle ways, as when a garlic clove is heated in oil so that it imparts a mild flavour, but removed before other ingredients are added to the pan.

ABOVE: *Garlic.*

GINGER

Valued not just as an aromatic, but also for its medicinal qualities, ginger is used throughout China. Commonly referred to as a root, ginger is actually a rhizome, or underground stem. When young, it is juicy and tender, with a sharp flavour suggestive of citrus. At this stage it can easily be sliced, chopped or pounded to a paste. Older roots are tougher and may need to be peeled and grated.

CHILLIES

Although they did not originate in Asia, chillies have been embraced so fervently there that they are now irrevocably associated with the area, including China. They are fundamental to Sichuan cooking and are also used in other regional cuisines, but it is for their flavour rather than their fire that they are most valued.

LEMON GRASS

A perennial tufted plant with a bulbous base, lemon grass looks like a plump spring onion (scallion) and doesn't seem very promising as an ingredient until the stalk is cut or bruised. It is only then that the lively, but not acidic, citrus aroma becomes evident. There are two main ways of using lemon grass. The stalk can be kept whole, bruised, then cooked slowly in liquid until it releases its flavour and is removed, or the tender lower portion of the stalk can be finely sliced or chopped and then added to stir-fries.

ABOVE: *Red chillies.*

RICE VINEGAR

Vinegar fermented from rice, or distilled from rice grains, is used extensively in Chinese and East Asian cooking. The former is dark amber in colour and is referred to in China as red or black vinegar; the latter is clear, so it is called white vinegar. Unless labelled yonezu (pure rice vinegar), most Japanese vinegars, called su or kokumotsu-su (grain vinegar), contain other grains besides rice.

RICE WINE

Chinese rice wine is generally known as huang jiu (yellow wine) in Chinese, because of its golden amber colour. The best quality rice wine is Shaohsing, named after the district where it is made. Its distinctive flavour is fragrant and smoky, and it is added to food at the end of cooking so that its aroma is retained.

ABOVE: *Rice wine.*

SOY SAUCE

Soy sauce is made from fermented soya beans, and is one of Asia's most important contributions to the global pantry. It is used all over the world, not merely as a condiment in place of salt, but as an ingredient in a host of home-made and manufactured foods. There are three types of Chinese soy sauce on the market. Light soy sauce is the initial extraction, like the first pressing of virgin olive oil. It has the most delicate flavour and is light brown in colour with a lovely "beany" fragrance. Dark soy sauce is left to mature further, and has caramel added to it, so it is slightly sweeter and has a much darker colour and a powerful aroma. Then there is the regular soy sauce, which is a blend of the two. As a rule, light soy sauce is used for seafood, white meats,

ABOVE: *Hoisin, plum and oyster sauce.*

vegetables and soups, while the darker sauce is ideal for red meats, stews, barbecues and gravy. If you are serving soy sauce as a dip, choose the regular variety, or use a blend of three parts light sauce with two parts dark. This proportion also applies to marinades.

OYSTER SAUCE

Oyster sauce is a Cantonese speciality. This thick, brown, soy-based sauce is flavoured with oyster juice, salt and caramel, and is thickened with cornflour (cornstarch). It is thicker than soy sauce and fish sauce, but lighter in colour. It has a pleasant, fragrant aroma, and a delicious and delicate flavour that, surprisingly, doesn't taste of fish at all. Oyster sauce is a highly versatile flavouring and can be used in a wide variety of dishes. It is especially good with fairly bland foods, such as chicken and tofu, but also works very well with more strongly flavoured ingredients such as beef and seafood. It can be used as a condiment at the table and is often sprinkled over the top of cooked dishes such as rice and noodles. Vegetarian varieties, made from mushrooms, are also available.

ABOVE: *Dark and light soy sauce.*

ABOVE: *Oyster sauce.*

HOISIN SAUCE

Another Cantonese speciality, hoisin is also known as barbecue sauce. Its Chinese name literally means "sea-flavour", which is a reflection on just how delicious it is, rather than an indication of its ingredients. Hoisin sauce does not contain so much as a trace of seafood, unlike oyster sauce and fish sauce. The main components of this very popular sauce are fermented beans, sugar, vinegar, salt, chilli, garlic and sesame oil, but there is no standard formula, so the aroma and flavour of different brands can vary considerably. A good quality product should have a fragrant aroma with a rich, warm, sweet yet salty flavour.

PLUM SAUCE

Made from plum juice with sugar, salt, vinegar and a thickening agent, plum sauce is a sweet-and-sour sauce. There is no standard recipe for the commercially made plum sauce. The various brands all seem to use slightly different seasonings and some even add garlic, ginger or chilli to give it extra tang. Taste before use, as some brands can be quite fiery. One of the common uses for plum sauce in the West is to serve it with Peking duck. It is also used as a dip for dim sum.

BLACK BEAN SAUCE

A mixture of puréed salted black beans with soy sauce, sugar and spices, this popular sauce is especially manufactured for the convenience of Western cooks, since people in China and South-east Asia generally use only whole fermented beans, and make their own sauce by crushing the beans in the wok while cooking. Fermented black beans have a powerful "fragrance" and a strong flavour that does not always appeal to the untutored Western palate, but once introduced to its rather earthy taste, many people grow to like it immensely.

YELLOW BEAN SAUCE

Also known as brown bean sauce or ground bean sauce, this Chinese favourite consists of crushed fermented soya beans which have been mixed with salt, wheat flour and sugar to make a paste which is not only useful on its own, but is also the basis of numerous more elaborate sauces. Hoisin sauce, chu hou sauce, Guilin chilli sauce, Sichuan hot sauce and Peking duck sauce all owe their ancestry to yellow bean sauce.

RED BEAN PASTE

Made from either red kidney beans or aduki beans, this is a thick, smooth paste, which is sweetened with rock sugar. The paste has a pleasant, mild fragrance and a subtle flavour. Although it is sweetened, the sauce is never cloying, and Asian cooks often add extra sugar to intensify the flavour. Occasionally, other flavourings such as essence of sesame seeds or ground cassia are blended in.

ABOVE: *Red bean pastes.*

LEFT: *Yellow bean, oyster, black bean, light soy, dark soy and hoisin sauces.*

Oils and fats

Although the design of a Chinese wok means that oil is the ingredient you need least of – unless you are deep-frying – the type you use is important because of the high temperatures involved.

GROUNDNUT OIL

Also known as peanut oil, this type of oil is ideal for use in Chinese cooking, especially in a wok. It reaches a high temperature without smoking and has a neutral flavour that won't mask the taste of the food. Like olive oil, groundnut oil is monounsaturated, although it does contain a slightly higher percentage of saturated fat than corn oil or sunflower oil. Some people can be allergic to groundnut oil, so make sure you inform guests if you have used it for cooking.

CORN OIL

Extracted from the germ of the corn kernel, this polyunsaturated oil is almost tasteless, although it can have a discernible odour. It is very good for both stir-frying and deep-frying since it can withstand high heat without reaching smoking point.

LARD

Although this animal fat is no longer widely used for frying in the West, due to health implications, it remains a common cooking medium in parts of China. The disadvantage of using lard, other than it being a saturated fat, is that it is often strongly flavoured.

RAPESEED (CANOLA) OIL

This monounsaturated oil is particularly popular in North America, but also lends itself well to Chinese cooking. It is pale gold in colour and has a mild flavour and aroma. The smoking point is slightly lower than corn oil, but it is regarded as a good choice for stir-frying and deep-frying.

SESAME OIL

Light sesame oil can be used for frying, but the dark type made from roasted sesame seeds is largely used for flavouring. It has a nutty taste, which becomes more pronounced if the oil is warmed. It mustn't be

ABOVE: *Sunflower and groundnut oil.*

allowed to get too hot, though, or it will burn. A few drops of sesame oil are often added to soup, noodles or a stir-fry before serving.

SUNFLOWER OIL

Another much-used polyunsaturated oil, this has a mild flavour. With a smoking point that rivals that of corn oil and groundnut oil, it is a very good choice for wok cooking.

WOK OIL

This product, specially developed for the wok, combines soya and sesame oils and is flavoured with ginger, garlic and pepper. It's an expensive way to start a stir-fry, but gives good results and is convenient if you have little time.

ABOVE: *Rapeseed oil.*

Tofu and soya

Tofu, an inexpensive protein food made from soya beans, was invented by the Chinese. It is now widely used throughout the world as an alternative to fish and meat.

When it comes to wok cooking, tofu and similar soya products score on several fronts. They are nutritious, easy to use and need little or no cooking. Although most forms are virtually tasteless, they take on surrounding flavours, so are useful for adding bulk while boosting food values. Tofu is low in fat and cholesterol-free.

The process of making tofu is not unlike making cheese, only much less time-consuming. The soya beans are soaked, husked, then pounded with water to make soya milk. The mixture is then filtered, boiled and finally curdled with gypsum.

SILKEN TOFU

This white product is the most delicate form of tofu. A creamy version comes in tubs and can be used for dips or desserts, including a non-dairy ice cream.

The slightly firmer type of silken tofu comes in cubes, which break down easily, so must be handled gently. If you use silken tofu cubes in a stir-fry, add them right at the end and don't toss the mixture too vigorously as this can cause the tofu to break up.

LEFT: *Textured Vegetable Protein.*

FIRM TOFU

This lightly pressed product is sold in cakes or blocks, either submerged in water or vacuum-packed, and can be cubed or sliced. It makes a good addition to a stir-fry, especially when marinated in soy sauce with strong flavours such as ginger, garlic or fermented black beans.

FRIED TOFU

At first glance, this doesn't look much like tofu. Slice the nut-brown block, however, and the white interior is exposed. The outer colour is the result of deep-frying in vegetable oil, a process that not only adds flavour, but also makes the tofu more robust. Fried tofu won't break down when cooked.

TVP/TEXTURED VEGETABLE PROTEIN

This meat substitute is made from soya flour from which the fat has been removed. It can be flavoured and shaped to mimic minced (ground) beef and is also sold in cubes or slices. The very low fat content of TVP means that it keeps well even without refrigeration.

TOFU SKINS

Dried tofu skins have neither flavour nor aroma until cooked, when they will rapidly absorb the flavour of seasonings and sauces. They need to be soaked in water before use.

ABOVE: *Silken and firm tofu and tofu skins.*

ABOVE: *Fried tofu.*

Rice and noodles

These low-fat, high-carbohydrate foods are immensely important in China and East Asia, forming the bulk of most meals. People in the north of China favour noodles, while those in the south prefer rice. Japanese and Korean cooks make excellent use of both.

RICE

Many Chinese people eat rice three times a day and it is no coincidence that the Chinese character for cooked rice, 'fan', also stands for nourishment and good health. Rice is the essential element of the meal and anything served with it is secondary. Rice is a non-allergenic food, rich in complex carbohydrates and low in salts and fats. It contains small amounts of easily digestible protein, together with phosphorus, magnesium, potassium and zinc. Brown rice, which retains the bran, yields vitamin E and some B-group vitamins, and is also a source

ABOVE: *Rice noodles.*

of fibre. Although it is healthier than white rice, it is the latter that is preferred in East Asia.

There are thousands of varieties of rice, many of which are known only in the areas where they are cultivated. The simplest method of classification is by the length of the grain, which can be long, medium or short. Long grain rice is three or four times as long as it is wide. When cooked, the individual grains remain separate. If the rice is medium grain, cooking will cause the grains to soften and start to cling together. This is even more marked in short grain rice, which absorbs liquid during cooking and becomes sticky and creamy. Glutinous rice has grains that stick together exceptionally well. In China, the everyday rice is a long grain variety, xian, but geng, a glutinous rice, is used for puddings and dim sum.

ABOVE: *Black and white glutinous rice.*

ABOVE: *Different thicknesses of egg noodles.*

NOODLES

Second only to rice as a staple food, noodles are enjoyed throughout China. Usually mixed with other ingredients such as vegetables or seafood, rather than being served solo as an accompaniment, noodles are eaten at all times of day and are a popular breakfast food. Chinese noodles are made from flours from a wide range of sources, including wheat, rice, mung bean, buckwheat, seaweed and devil's tongue, which is a plant related to the arum lily. Some noodles are plain, others are enriched with egg. They are sold fresh and dried.

Wheat noodles are made from water, wheat flour and salt. Egg noodles, which are enriched wheat noodles, are extremely popular. They are made in various thicknesses and may be fresh or dried, in coils or blocks.

Cellophane noodles consist of very fine, clear strands. They are also known as mung bean noodles, transparent noodles, bean-thread noodles or glass noodles. When cooked, they remain firm, and it is their texture, rather than their bland taste, that appeals.

Rice noodles come in various forms, from very thin strands called rice vermicelli to flattened sheets.

Cooking rice and noodles

Many Chinese recipes are based on rice or noodles, which may be used as an accompaniment rather than part of the main dish. If you are using your wok for the accompaniment, you will probably be cooking your rice or noodles in a separate pan.

COOKING RICE

There are several ways of cooking rice, but the absorption method is best for jasmine, basmati, short grain and glutinous rice. As a guide, you will need about 600ml/1 pint/2½ cups water for every 225g/8oz/generous 1 cup rice.

1 Rinse the rice thoroughly and put it in a pan. Pour in the water. Do not add salt. Bring to the boil, then reduce the heat to the lowest possible setting.

2 Cover and cook for 20–25 minutes, or until the liquid is absorbed. Without lifting the lid, remove the pan from the heat. Leave to stand for 5 minutes to finish cooking.

Steamed sticky rice

Sticky rice is commonly used in Chinese desserts. To get the authentic texture steam it in a bamboo steamer. Make sure you buy the right type of rice – usually called sticky or glutinous rice.

1 Rinse the rice several times, then soak overnight in cold water. Line a bamboo steamer with muslin (cheesecloth). Drain the rice and spread out evenly on the muslin.

2 Cover the steamer and steam for 25–30 minutes, until tender.

ABOVE: *Bamboo steamed sticky rice.*

COOKING NOODLES

When cooking noodles, check the packet for instructions. Par-cooked noodles only need to be soaked in hot water; others must be boiled. Ready-to-use noodles are simply added to a stir-fry and tossed over the heat until hot.

Preparing rice noodles

Rice noodles are par-cooked when you buy them, so they only need to be soaked in hot water before use. Add the noodles to a large bowl of just-boiled water and leave for 5–10 minutes or until softened, stirring occasionally to separate.

Preparing wheat noodles

Wheat noodles take very little time. Add the noodles to a pan of boiling water and cook for 2–4 minutes, until tender. Drain well. If they are going to be cooked further in a stir-fry, give the noodles just 2 minutes initially.

Pancakes and wrappers

Duck-filled pancakes, crispy wontons and moreish spring rolls are synonymous with Chinese cuisine and relatively simply to create at home if you have the correct ingredients.

PANCAKES

Chinese pancakes are almost always made from plain dough, rather than a batter, and are more often served with savoury fillings rather than sweet.

There are two types of pancakes in China, either thin or thick varieties. Thin pancakes (bobing) are also known as Mandarin or duck pancakes, because they are used as wrappers for serving the famous Peking duck. They are also served with other savoury dishes, most notably the very popular mu-shu or moo-soo pork.

Making pancakes demands considerable dexterity, so many cooks prefer to buy them frozen from the Chinese supermarket.

Thick pancakes are made with lard and flavoured with savoury ingredients such as spring onions (scallions) and rock salt. In northern China, they are eaten as a snack, or as part of a main meal. Both thin and thick pancakes are sometimes served as a dessert, with a filling of sweetened bean paste.

SPRING ROLL WRAPPERS

Spring rolls are called egg rolls in the United States, and pancake rolls in many other parts of the world. They must be one of the most popular Chinese snacks everywhere, including China itself. While the fillings may vary from region to region, or even between different restaurants and fast food stalls, the wrappers are always more or less the same. They are made

ABOVE: *Spring roll wrappers.*

from a simple wheat flour and water dough, except in Vietnam, where they use rice flour, water and salt.

There are three different sizes of ready-made spring roll wrappers available from the freezers of Asian stores: small, medium and large. They are all wafer-thin. The smallest wrappers, which are about 12cm/4½in square, are used for making dainty, cocktail-style rolls. The standard-size wrappers measure 21–23cm/8½–9in square, and usually come in packets of 20 sheets. The largest, 30cm/12in square, are too big for general use, so they are usually cut in half or into strips for making samosas and similar snacks.

Reheating Chinese pancakes

1 If the pancakes are frozen then defrost them thoroughly. Peel the pancakes apart and restack them, placing a small square of baking parchment between each one. Use as many pancakes as are necessary.

2 Carefully wrap the stacked pancakes in foil, folding over the sides of the foil. Ensure that the pancakes are completely sealed within the foil, as this will help them retain the heat while they are steaming.

3 Put the foil parcel in a bamboo steamer and cover with the lid. Place the steamer on a trivet in a wok of simmering water. Steam for 3–5 minutes until the pancakes are heated through.

ABOVE: *Wonton wrappers.*

WONTON SKINS

Wonton skins or wrappers are made from a flour and egg dough, which is rolled out to a smooth, thin sheet, as when making egg noodles. The sheet is usually cut into small squares, although round wonton wrappers are also available. Ready-made wonton skins are stacked in piles of 25 or 50, wrapped and sold fresh or frozen.

Unlike spring roll wrappers, which have to be carefully peeled off sheet by sheet before use, fresh wonton skins are dusted with flour before being packed. This keeps each one separate from the others and so they are very easy to use. Frozen wrappers must, however, be thawed thoroughly before use, or they will tend to stick together. Any unused skins can be re-frozen, but should be carefully wrapped in foil so that they do not dry out in the freezer.

There are several ways of using wonton skins. They can be deep-fried and served with a dip, filled and boiled, steamed or deep-fried, or simply poached in a clear broth. On most Chinese restaurant menus in the West, this last option is listed under soups, which is misleading, as in China and South-east Asia wonton soup is always served solo as a snack, never as a separate soup course as part of a meal.

Preparing wontons

Place the filling in the centre of the wonton skin and dampen the edges. Press the edges of the wonton skin together to create a little purse shape, sealing the filling completely.

Preparing spring rolls

Spring roll wrappers should be thawed before use. Fill with ingredients such as beansprouts, bamboo shoots, water chestnuts and dried mushrooms, with chopped prawns (shrimp). When the rolls are prepared, deep-fry them a few at a time in hot oil for 2–3 minutes, or until golden and crisp.

2 Spoon the spring roll filling diagonally across the wrapper.

4 Brush the edges with cornflour (cornstarch) and water paste.

1 Peel off the top spring roll wrapper. Cover the rest to keep them moist.

3 Fold over the nearest corner of the wrapper to cover the filling.

5 Fold the edges towards the middle, then roll up into a neat parcel.

Dumplings

Very popular in China, dumplings are available in a wide variety of different shapes and sizes, with fillings ranging from pork and vegetables to mushrooms and bamboo shoots. Some enclose the filling in a very thin dough skin (jiao zi) while others use a dough made from a glutinous rice flour. There are also steamed buns (bao zi) filled with meat or a sweet bean paste.

The best way to experience the diversity and delicious flavours of dumplings is to indulge in dim sum, that wonderful procession of tasty morsels that the Cantonese have elevated to an art form. Although dumplings originated in northern China, it was in Canton that the practice developed of enjoying these snacks with tea at breakfast or lunch time.

Dim sum literally means "dot on the heart" and indicates a snack or refreshment, not a full-blown meal. Although the range of dishes available on a dim sum menu now embraces other specialities (spring rolls, wontons and spare ribs, for instance), dumplings remain the essential items. What is more, unlike the majority of dim sum, which are so complicated to make that they can only be prepared by a highly skilled chef, dumplings are comparatively simple to make at home. Both jiao zi and bao zi are available ready-made from Asian or Chinese stores – the former are sold uncooked and frozen, and the latter are ready-cooked and sold chilled.

PREPARATION AND COOKING TECHNIQUES

Frozen jiao zi dumplings should be cooked straight from the freezer. There are three different ways of cooking and serving them.

Poaching

The most common way of cooking dumplings in China is to poach them in boiling water for 4–5 minutes – longer if cooking from frozen. The dumplings are added to boiling water. When the water boils again, a cupful of cold water is added to the pan and the water is brought to the boil again. This is repeated twice more, by which time the dumplings will be ready. They are traditionally served hot with a vinegar and soy sauce dip, chilli sauce or chilli oil.

ABOVE: *Crispy griled (broiled) dumplings.*

Steaming

The traditional way to do this is by using a bamboo steamer, placed over a wok of boiling water. The dumplings are placed on a bed of lettuce or spinach leaves on the rack of the steamer, which is then covered. The dumplings are served hot with a dip.

Grilling/broiling

This description is a bit misleading, because the dumplings are not grilled (broiled) in the conventional sense but cooked in a shallow wok. They are first shallow-fried, then a small amount of boiling water is added to the pan and they are steamed under cover until all the liquid has evaporated. When cooked by this method, the dumplings are crispy on the base, soft on top and juicy inside. They are often called by their popular name, which is "pot stickers".

Cooking dumplings

1 To poach dumplings, drop them into boiling water. When the water boils again, add a cupful of cold water. Repeat twice more, cooking the dumplings for 4–5 minutes.

2 To steam dumplings, place them on a bed of lettuce or spinach leaves on the base of a bamboo **steamer**, cover with the lid and cook for 8–10 minutes.

3 To "grill" ("broil") dumplings, fry in a shallow wok until they are brown, then add a little water, cover with a bamboo steamer lid, and cook until the water has completely evaporated.

Peking dumplings

These crescent-shaped dumplings are filled with minced (ground) pork, greens and spring onions (scallions) and seasoned with salt, sugar, soy sauce, rice wine and sesame oil. In northern China they are eaten for breakfast on New Year's Day, but are often served all year round as snacks or part of a meal.

Steamed buns

Steamed buns are to Asia what baked bread is to the West, and bao (filled buns) are the Chinese fast food equivalent of hot dogs, hamburgers and sandwiches. There are two main types of steamed buns, either plain or filled. The plain, unfilled buns made from leavened dough are treated in much the same way as plain boiled rice and are intended to be eaten with cooked food. Then there are filled buns (bao zi). The name literally means "wraps" and these can be savoury or sweet. The sweet ones contain either a lotus seed paste or a sweet bean paste filling and are usually eaten cold. Savoury bao zi come with a wide range of fillings, the most common being pork, and a very popular type is filled with Cantonese

BELOW: *Steamed buns.*

ABOVE: *Prawn crackers.*

char siu (honey-roasted pork). These are available ready-made, and are best eaten hot.

Also available ready-made, but uncooked, are what are known as Shanghai dumplings. These are little round dumplings, much smaller than char siu bao, each consisting of minced (ground) pork wrapped in a thin skin of unleavened dough.

Prawn crackers

Also called shrimp chips, prawn crackers are made from fresh prawns (shrimp), starch, salt and sugar. They are very popular as cocktail snacks, and some restaurants serve them while you wait for your order to arrive. The raw crackers are grey in colour. The small Chinese ones are not much bigger than a thumbnail, while those used in Indonesia are much larger, about 15cm/6in long and 5cm/2in wide. Indonesian prawn crackers are more difficult to find in the West. Once deep-fried, both types puff up to four or five times the original size, and become almost snow white. Ready-cooked crackers are also available. They are sold in sealed packets, but do not keep well once exposed to the air, so eat them as soon as possible after opening.

Index